The
Western Cherokee Nation
Of
Arkansas and Missouri

A History

A Heritage

Doyne "Two Wolves" Cantrell

With the counsel of::

Senior Elder Ben "Little Eagle" Stephens

ISBN: 978-0-557-07892-9

Published by Lulu Publishing

2009

Printed in the United States of America

Acknowledgement

The work of putting together this book has been a labor of love for our people, the Western Cherokee Nation of Arkansas and Missouri. It has been a great honor and privilege to work with the many members who have contributed to this project. They have become good friends for life and trusted confidants as well.

First and foremost, I must thank my God and Savior for bringing me to this time and place in life to be a part of this great Nation.

Thanks to our Ancestors who have gone before us and blazed the paths and trail that we follow today in our traditions and culture. Our heritage has made this work possible. Men like Major Ridge, John Boudinot, Stand Watie, and many others have forged the heritage that we today have reclaimed.

Ben "Little Eagle" Stephens, our senior Elder, has been invaluable in contributing to this work and lending direction in compilation. He truly is a Cherokee that loves Cherokees. Without his counsel and guidance, this book would never have become the work that it is.

Tom "Red Feather" Ward has given a great deal of direction in the technical aspects of publishing as well as contributing much to the work contained herein. As a published author with several books in print, his expertise, knowledge, and wisdom have been a great asset to our work on this project.

My sincere and deepest thanks go out to Annette Welch for her contribution in the editing of this work and for the inclusion of some of her familial traditional herbal remedies. Her expertise and experience has been of great value without which this work would not have been completed.

The encouragement of Pam Davis has been a great inspiration and motivator to keep me on track with this project.

Rod Otter Johnson, a good friend and strong supporter of our nation, has helped to keep me focused on primary information. The difficulty of documenting the facts has been easier because of Otter's contributions. Thank you, Otter, for your work on this project and your friendship.

I especially thank my wonderful wife, Debra, for the sacrifice of many family hours as I huddled in my cubbyhole to work on this project. She is the greatest and most supportive friend and partner for which one could ask. God has truly blessed me with her companionship. I love you Debra.

Thank you all.

Doyne Cantrell

Dedication

     This book is dedicated to the memory of the many who have suffered to preserve our heritage that is rich in culture, tradition, and love. Among those to whom we dedicate this work are the previous chiefs of the Western Cherokee Nation of Arkansas and Missouri who are also known as the Old Settlers.

(1795-1813)	Di wa li also known as The Bowl
(1813-1817)	Tonkatoka
(1817-1819)	Tahlonteeskee
(1819-1838)	John Jolly
(1838-1839)	John Looney
(1839)	John Brown
(1840)	John Rogers

     From the years 1840 to 1998, with the cessation of John Rogers as chief, the tribal Elders served as the leadership of the Nation unifying and leading the people known as the Western Cherokee or the Old Settlers. We dedicate this work to them.

Ben Little Eagle Stephens

Table of Contents

Forward

The history of our tribe is a work in progress. It requires many hours of research and input by so many people. Why do we do what we do? Maybe the following poem will help to answer that question.

WE ARE THE CHOSEN

My feelings are that in each tribe, we are called to find the Ancestors.

We put flesh on their bones and make them live again.

We tell the tribe's story and feel that somehow the Ancestors know and approve.

To me, researching genealogy is not a cold gathering of facts, but it

is the breathing of life into all who have gone before.

We are the storytellers of the tribe.

We have been called as it were by our genes.

Those who have gone before cry out to us:

"Tell our story".....So, we do.

In finding them, we somehow find ourselves.

How many graves have I stood before now and cried?

I have lost count.

How many times have I told the ancestors, "You have a wonderful family?"

You would be proud of us.

How many times have I walked up to a grave and felt?

Somehow there was love for me there. I cannot say.

It goes beyond just documenting facts. It goes to who I am, and why I do the things that I do.

It goes to seeing a cemetery about to be lost forever to weeds of indifference and saying, "I can't let this happen."

The bones lying here are bones of my bones and flesh of my flesh.

It goes to pride in what our Ancestors were able to accomplish

and their contributions to what we are today.

It goes to respecting their hardships and losses.

They never gave up.

Through resoluteness, they endured and built a life for their families and our tribe.

It goes to deep pride that they fought to make and keep us a Nation.

It goes to a deep and immense understanding that they were doing it for us in the hope

that we might be born whom we are and remember our ancestors. So, we do remember with love, caring, and the scribing of each fact of their existence.

We are they and they are we.

So as a scribe who has been called, I tell the story of my tribe.

It is up to the one called in the next generation

to answer and take my place

in the long line of tribal storytellers.

This is why I do our tribal history.

That is what called all those young and old

to step up and put flesh on the bones.

Submitted by Redfeather

A Brief History of the Old Settler Cherokee

In the late 1700's, some of the Cherokee people from the Lookout Mountain area of Tennessee moved west of the Mississippi River into the Arkansas Territory. They first settled in the Lansing and Cape Girardeau, Missouri, areas. Later, they settled in what is now Greene and Poinsett Counties in Arkansas. Eventually, they settled along the St. Francis River in southeast Missouri and in northeast Arkansas. Only a few years later, there were more than 1000 living along the Illinois and Arkansas Rivers near what are now Russellville and Dardanelle.

In 1817, settlers of the Spanish-American trading posts in the Arkansas Territory estimated that there were in excess of 5000 Cherokee warriors dispersed along the Arkansas, White, and St. Francis Rivers.

With the Turkey Town Treaty of July 8, 1817, land in the East was exchanged for land in northwest Arkansas just north of the Arkansas River and south of the White River. This treaty gave hope to the Western Cherokee of Arkansas and Missouri that they would be able to protect their holdings thereby creating a new homeland in northwest Arkansas. However, many of the Eastern Cherokee saw the treaty as a betrayal. It is estimated that as many as 4,000 Cherokee may have come west to join the Western Cherokee Nation. Included in these were parties of families led by Principal Chief John Jolly, who was the brother of Tolluntuskee; Dick Justice, also known as Dek-keh the Just;

the Glass, Walter "Wat" Weber; John Rogers; John Graves, and John and David Brown. In 1829, Sequoyah, also known as George Gist or Guest, invented the Cherokee syllabary.

Some of the major figures of the Western Cherokee included Black Fox, Dutch, Spring Frog, and Takatoka. Some tribal members eventually moved to the area of the Red River including some groups lead by Du-wa-li (known as The Bowl). Later, the groups were lead by Dutch.

Di wa li (The Bowl) was one of the first chiefs of the Western Cherokee Old Settlers. Chief Toluntuskee followed him. It was Toluntuskee who invited missionaries to come to the area where they lived in Arkansas. When he died, his brother, John Jolly, became chief. John Looney and John Brown followed Chief John Jolly as chief. During John Brown's tenure as chief, the final group of Eastern Cherokee came through the Trail of Tears into the Old Settler's lands.

The British naturalist, Thomas Nuttall, described the Arkansas Cherokee well when in 1819 he traveled up the Arkansas River: "....both banks of the river, as we proceeded, were lined with the houses and farms of the Cherokees, and their dress was a mixture of indigenous and European taste, yet in their houses, which are decently furnished, and in their farms, which were well fenced and stocked with cattle ... argue a propitius [sic] progress in their population. Their superior industry, either as hunters or farmers, proves the value of property among them." Nuttall met John Jolly and his wife on April 9, 1819. He stated, "I should scarcely have distinguished him from an American, except by his language. He was very plain, prudent, and unassuming in his dress and manners; a Franklin among his countrymen, and affectionately called the beloved father."[i]

The Cherokee that remained in the East lost all their old homelands upon their forced removal through the illegal Treaty of 1835. This treaty dispossessed the Western Cherokee of Arkansas, as well as the early immigrants of 1817. They were to be granted an acre for acre exchange of the land west of the land they already owned and occupied. Later, a small amount of land was restored through the benevolence of a local citizen, William Thomas, to a small group located in present day Cherokee, North Carolina. This group was known as the Eastern Band of Cherokee Indians. Some of their eastern cousins were relocated in eastern Oklahoma and are known as the Cherokee Nation of Oklahoma. A wide remnant of people with Cherokee ancestry can be found today in every state. Many can be found in the South.

John Ross, the principal chief of the Eastern Cherokee, was among the last group of the Immigrants to arrive in the western lands. There was a great deal of political unrest between the immigrant group and the Old Settlers. Chief Brown called a meeting to formally welcome the Immigrants to their new country. Cephas Washburn, a missionary, was present at the meetings. He reported that the Immigrants and the Old Settlers made congratulatory speeches on their reunion as one nation. They expressed the hope that nothing like this would ever occur again. When John Brown was announcing the closing of this meeting, John Ross asked what the terms would be for receiving the Immigrants. Brown explained that they had been received, and all seemed accepting of the reception. Ross, however, wanted a more formal reception and asked for the Old Settlers to detail the privileges for which they would be entitled. Chief Brown made another speech in which he did outline their reception in terms that were cordial and accepting. Washburn reported Chief Brown as saying,

"We cordially receive you as brothers. We joyfully welcome you to our country. The whole land is before you. You may freely go where ever you choose and select any places for settlement which may please you, with this restriction that you do not interfere with the private rights of individuals. You are fully entitled to the elective franchise; are lawful voters in any of the districts in which you reside, and eligible to any of the offices within the gift of the people. Next October, according to the law the term of service of the Chiefs will expire and any of you are eligible to those seats. Next July will be an election in our district for members of both

houses of our legislature, for judges, sheriffs, etc. At those elections, you will be voters and you are eligible to any of those offices. A government was, many years since, organized in this country, and a code of laws was established, suited to our condition and under which our people have lived in peace and prosperity. It is expected that you will all be subject to our government and laws until they shall be constitutionally altered or repealed and that in all this you will demean yourselves as good and peaceable citizens."

Most responded positively to the speech, but Ross wanted his people to remain an organized body politic for the purpose of settling their accounts with the government and securing their claims. Washburn wrote that Brown replied,

"For the settlement of all matters growing out of your removal from the old nation and for your subsistence for one year, and for the adjustment of all claims against the United States, you are freely allowed your own chiefs and committee and council, and judges and sheriff, with the name and style of the Eastern Cherokee nation."

After much discussion and disagreement, Chief Brown, at the end of his patience, adjourned the meeting. Ross called his own meeting to establish a new constitution and displace the current government. (It was during this time that the Ridge party was assassinated for their part in the negotiation of the Treaty of New Echota and removal from the East.) John Ross became chief of the (Oklahoma) Cherokee and began to systematically exclude the Old Settlers from government. The federal agents and the Washington officials called on Ross to resign as head of the Cherokee government, but he declined. He had profited from the Removal and became a very rich man. He and his brother, Lewis Ross, had negotiated a contract with the government to oversee the removal of all Cherokee from the East. He received millions of dollars for that contract.[ii]

Western Cherokee Old Settler Chiefs

In 1794, the first group of Cherokee fled to the valley of the St. Francis River in southeast Missouri. Their leader, The Bowl, was accused of leading a massacre on trespassers. Though later vindicated, he and his followers remained in the New Madrid area. In 1811, a massive earthquake caused the Mississippi River to flow backwards and for months tremors continued. Convinced the Great Spirit was displeased, the Western Cherokee moved to Arkansas. The Bowl remained chief until 1813 and was followed by Takatoka who became chief from 1813-18.

Led by Tahlonteeskee, three hundred others including Chief Takatoka migrated to Arkansas in 1809. The Bowl and his followers stayed in Arkansas until they decided to go to Texas in 1819-20. Takatoka resisted missionary efforts, but it was at his place on the Illinois Bayou in Arkansas that Sequoyah first taught the use of his syllabary.

On a trip to Washington City, Takatoka died at Kaskaskia, IL and Tahlonteeskee, an uncle of Sequoyah, became the third chief of the Western Cherokee Nation of Arkansas and Missouri. Tahlonteeskee and Doublehead were signers of a treaty in 1805 that labeled them traitors. Tahlonteeskee departed for the West. Doublehead remained and was later slain by Major Ridge. Ridge became a proponent of moving to the West and was slain by a faction that weren't in favor of the treaty made in 1805 after the Removal (Trail of Tears).

Tahlonteeskee, the first western chief to allow Christianity to come to the Cherokee, permitted missionaries to establish the Dwight Mission in Arkansas in response to the building of Fort Smith. Tahlonteeskee died in 1818. His brother, John Jolly, who had moved west in 1817, then became chief.

The Dwight Mission was the first American mission established for the Cherokee Indians west of the Mississippi River and was located near Russellville and Little Rock, Arkansas. The government had moved the Western Cherokee from their location in Georgia and Tennessee to Arkansas Territory after the Treaty of 1817. Reverend Cephas Washburn and Reverend Albert Finney, Rev. Washburn's brother-in-law, started the Dwight Mission in 1820. They were both from the Elliot Mission in Mississippi. The mission was started at the request of Chief Tahlonteeskee of the Western Cherokee. Chief Tahlonteeskee had been impressed with the school previously started for the Eastern Cherokee. The purpose of the Dwight Mission was to expose the Cherokee children to Christianity and to provide them with an education as well.

The early Cherokee migrated from Georgia, Tennessee, and Alabama and were called Arkansas or Cherokee West. The name distinguished them from their tribesmen who remained in the East. Later, they were referred to as "Old Settlers."

"Since 1827, the names of the elected Old Settler principal chiefs and secondary chiefs were recorded, but a listing of them is difficult to come by." *(Ancient Cherokee Rulers)* A list of the chiefs of the Arkansas Cherokee shows John Bowl, Takatoka, Tahlonteeskee, and John Jolly up to 1828. John Brown became one of the Old Settler chiefs along with John Looney and John Jolly. John Brown served as secondary chief to Chief Jolly. He became chief after Chief Jolly died at Webber Falls in December of 1838. He was head of the Old Settlers at the time the Eastern Cherokee chief, John Ross, arrived from the Trail of Tears in 1838.

"In new elections in the spring of 1839, John Brown, son of former Old Nation Chief Richard Brown, was named principal chief while John Looney and John Rogers were selected as second and third chiefs, respectively." *(Cherokee Nation - Reunion & Conflict)* Chief John Brown's reign did not last very long. On November 10, 1839, the Old Settlers denied any recognition of Ross's authority. Next, Ross deposed John Brown.

John Brown, who had been principal chief of the Western Cherokee of Arkansas and Missouri when the Ross party arrived, became so discouraged about the future of his people that he left for Mexico with his family and some friends. In Mexico, he intended to join the refugee Texas Cherokee. Back in Arkansas, the Old Settlers held the council in Tahlonteeskee *(a town named for the former chief)* and refused to accept the new Ross government.

John Rogers was elected the new principal chief. A civil war was brewing among the Cherokee.

President James K. Polk sent a three-man commission to the Cherokee in 1844. By then, John Brown had returned from Mexico. He was present at the meeting along with 286 Old Settlers and 179 Treaty Party members. John Ross was invited but declined to attend.

John Jolly, who followed Chief Toluntuskee, died while the latecomers were arriving, and John Looney automatically became chief. Looney was deposed by the council and replaced with John Brown. This was done with the idea of putting the Western Cherokee Nation in a better position vis-à-vis the Ross party. After the murders of Major Ridge, John Ridge, and Elias Boudinot (Treaty party members who supported the Old Settlers) in June of 1839, the council had a change of heart about resisting Ross's autocratic demands and deposed Brown replacing him with Looney. A sizable faction of the Old Settlers refused to recognize Looney and re-elected Rogers in his stead, but their efforts to maintain autonomy failed the next year.

The Bowl (1795-1813) Di wa li, the son of John Bowls, known as The Bowl, was a noted Cherokee chief and leader of one of the first bands to establish themselves permanently on the west side of the Mississippi. As the leader of some hostile Cherokee from the Chickamauga towns, he massacred all of the male members of a party of emigrants at Muscle Shoals, Tennessee, in 1794. After the massacre, he retired up the St. Francis River on the west side of the Mississippi. The Cherokee council, who offered to assist in his arrest, disowned his act. He remained in that region until after the cession of the Louisiana Territory to the United States. About 1824, so much dissatisfaction was caused by the delay in adjusting the boundaries of the territory of the Western Cherokee in Arkansas and the withholding of their annuities, that a party headed by Bowl crossed the Sabine River into Texas where they were joined by groups of refugees from a number of other eastern tribes. They began negotiations with the Mexican government for a tract of land on the Angelina, Neches, and Trinity Rivers. They were interrupted from this endeavor by the outbreak of the Texas War for Independence in 1835. Houston, who had long been a friend to the Cherokee people, entered into a treaty to assign them certain lands along the Angelina River. The Texas Senate rejected the treaty in 1837, and Houston's successor, Lamar, declared his intention to drive all Indians from Texas. On the plea that the Indians were entering into a conspiracy with the Mexican inhabitants, a commission supported by several regiments of troops was sent to the Cherokee town on the Angelina River to demand that they remove at once across the border. On their refusal, they were attacked on July 15-16, 1839, and defeated in two engagements. Bowl and his assistant chief, Hard-mush, were among the many killed. *See Mooney in 19th Rep. B. A. E., 1900. (J. R. S.)*

Chief Frank Bowles
by Oscar Berhain

The Bowl

Tonkatoka (1813-1817) Degadoga, or Tonkatoka, was an early Cherokee emigrant. He replaced The Bowl as principal chief of the Cherokee Nation West upon his departure for Spanish Texas in 1813. Tonkatoka served as the war chief of the Western Cherokee during the Cherokee-Osage War of 1817-1823 and was replaced as principal chief in 1817 by Tahlonteeskee,

Tahlonteeskee (1817-1819) Tollunteeskee requested that the American Board of Commissioners for Foreign Missions establish a mission in the west in 1818. Subsequently, Dwight Mission, near present Russellville, AR was established in the spring of 1820. He was the first western chief to allow Christianity to come to the Cherokee.

Sketch of Dwight Mission at Russellville (Pope County) 1824

From *Historic Arkansas*, courtesy of the Butler Center for Arkansas Studies, Central Arkansas Library System

In the mean time, Tahlonteeskee died and his brother, John Jolly who was the adopted father of Sam Houston, became chief. John Jolly had moved west in 1818.

Tahlonteeskee, brother or brother-in-law of Doublehead, was one of the best-known warriors of the Chickamauga Wars. John Watts told Governor William Blount that Tahlonteeskee was his uncle ("of a kind"), perhaps denoting a relationship by marriage. This older man named Tahlonteeskee was one of a Cherokee delegation to Philadelphia in 1791 along with Doublehead and Bloody Fellow. They met President George Washington. Later, Tahlonteeskee joined his nephew, John Watts, and along with young Dragging Canoe they made a secret trip to Pensacola, FL to get arms and supplies from a British merchant there. Governor Blount was informed of this trip by spy reports printed in the American State Papers.

The original town of Tahlonteeskee was named after him and became the first capitol of the Cherokee Nation in Indian Territory from 1828-1839. It is considered the oldest governmental capitol in Oklahoma, and it was operational in the Illinois district as a courthouse and meeting place for the Cherokee Nation.

John Jolly (1819-1838) Chief Jolly was noted as the adopted father of Gen. Samuel Houston and later chief of the Arkansas band of Cherokee. His native name was Ahúludégi, which means, "He throws away the drum." His early life was spent in Tennessee near the mouth of the Hiwassee where an island still preserves his name. It was here that Houston came to live with him. Houston remained 3 years and acquired a life long friendship for his adopted people, the Cherokee. In 1818, Jolly removed to the other side of the Mississippi and joined the Arkansas band. He became their chief a few years later on the death of Tollunteeskee. *Mooney in 19th Rep. B. A. E., 507, 1900.*

Chief Oo-loo-te-ka

(John Jolly…He- Puts the-Drum-Away)

John Looney (1838-1839) John Looney, with the consent of the whole tribe, was the last person elected principal chief of the Cherokee Nation West. It was his second election to that office. He was first elected to replace John Jolly after the latter died December 28, 1838, and he was deposed April 22, 1839, after the tribe elected John Brown in order to affect a union with the Latecomers from the Cherokee Nation East after the Cherokee Removal of 1838-1839.

He was elected to the office again in July when Brown and his officers were deposed for having failed to accomplish that task. He was removed from office again the next month when the reunited Cherokee Nation elected John Ross, with Joseph Vann as his assistant, as principal chief.

A dissident group of former members of the Cherokee Nation West elected John Rogers as their principal chief in October, but their efforts to maintain a separate organization fell apart the following year.

Looney was married to Betsy, daughter of Will Weber, the mixed-blood headman of Willstown during the Chickamauga wars. Also, Will Weber was the father-in-law of Stand Watie.

John Brown (1839) John Brown, formerly judge of the Chickamauga District of the Cherokee Nation East, was elected principal chief of the Cherokee Nation West on April 22, 1839, after the Old Settlers decided to elect new officers to strengthen their position vis-à-vis the Latecomers under John Ross. John Brown was elected in place of then Principal Chief John Looney. He served until a majority of the Old Settlers decided his administration had not gone far enough to accomplish a compromise with the Ross party. They re-elected his predecessor, John Looney, in July.

Chief John Brown

John Rogers (1839-1840) John Rogers was the last elected principal chief of the Cherokee Nation West. The faction of Old Settlers who rejected the Unity Constitution of September of 1839 elected him October 11, 1839. This faction gained no further adherents, and the effort died the next year. Rogers was the nephew of the Cherokee Nation West's principal chiefs, Tahlonteeskee and John Jolly.

Thomas Graves, George Maw, George Guess (Sequoya), Thomas Marvis, and John Rogers were noted as chiefs when the Treaty of 1828 was signed. The treaty was with the Western Cherokee for the exchange of their lands in Arkansas for the lands in Oklahoma, which was otherwise known as Indian Territory. Note that this was before the Trail of Tears.

Sequoya, although not an elected chief, was considered a very prominent figure in Cherokee history. He was the inventor of the Cherokee alphabet. He was born in the Cherokee town of Taskigi, TN about 1760. He died near San Fernando, Tamaulipas, Mexico, in August of 1843. He was the son of a white man and a Cherokee woman of mixed blood, a daughter of a chief in Echota. Besides his native name of Sikwayi, or Sequoya, he was known as George Gist, otherwise spelled Guest or Guess. His father was generally believed to have been a German trader. (He has also been claimed as the son of Nathaniel Gist of Revolutionary War note.)

Sequoya grew up in the tribe and was quite unacquainted with English, or civilized arts. He became a hunter and trader in furs. He was also a craftsman in silverwork and was an ingenious natural mechanic. His inventive powers had scope for development in consequence of an accident that befell him while hunting and rendered him a cripple for life. The importance of the arts of writing and printing as instruments and weapons of civilization began to impress him in 1809. He studied, undismayed by the discouragement and ridicule of his fellows, to elaborate a system of writing suitable to the Cherokee language. In 1821, he submitted his syllabary to the chief men of the nation. On their approval, Cherokee of all ages set about to learn the syllabary with such zeal that after a few months thousands were able to read and write the Cherokee language. In 1822, Sequoya visited Arkansas to introduce writing to the Western Cherokee. He made his permanent home with them in 1823. Parts of the Bible were printed in Cherokee in 1824. In 1828, The Cherokee Phoenix, a weekly newspaper published in both Cherokee and English, began to appear.

Sequoya was sent to Washington in 1828 as an envoy of the Arkansas band. He bore a conspicuous part in their affairs. When the Eastern Cherokee joined the Old Settlers in the west, Sequoya's influence and counsel were prominent in the organization of the reunited nation in Indian Territory. In his declining years, he withdrew from active political life and speculative ideas once again possessed his mind. He visited tribes of various stocks in a fruitless search for the elements of a common speech and grammar. He sought to trace a lost band of the Cherokee that according to tradition had crossed the Mississippi before the Revolution and wandered to some mountains in the west. While pursuing this quest in the Mexican sierras, he met his death. *See Mooney, Myths of the Cherokee, 19th Rep., B. A. E., 108 et seq., 147, 148, 1900, and the authorities therein cited. More on Sequoyah*

Stand Watie was born December 12, 1806, at the Cherokee town of Oothcaloga which is near present day Rome, GA. His Indian name was Degadoga, He Stands (on Two Feet). His Christian name was Isaac S. Watie, and he soon dropped his Christian name and became known as Stand Watie. His father was David Oowatie, and his mother was Susanna Reese, a white woman. He had two brothers, Buck Oowatie who was later known as Elias Boudinot and was the editor of the Cherokee newspaper, The Cherokee Phoenix. His younger brother was Thomas Oowatie.

The Watie family had large landholdings and ran a profitable ferry service on the Hightower River. The family was a member of the famous Ridge family that dominated Cherokee politics in the 1820's and 1830's. As early as 1828, Watie served as clerk of the Cherokee Supreme Court. He served for more than forty years as a practicing attorney within the Cherokee Nation.

In October of 1861, Watie received a commission as a colonel in the Army of the Confederacy. He joined forces with General Ben McCulloch's Texas Cavalry to raise a force to protect the Indian Territory from federal invasion by Kansas Jayhawkers. The fall of 1861, Confederates under the command of Colonel (later General) Douglas H. Cooper, the former Choctaw Indian agent from Mississippi, had assembled a formidable Indian force of 1,400 mounted men. This cavalry unit included six companies of Cooper's Choctaw and Chickasaw regiment, Colonel Daniel McIntosh's Creek regiment, and Lieutenant Chilly McIntosh and Major John Jumper's mixed battalion of Creeks and Seminoles. Five hundred white soldiers of the 9th Texas Calvary supported these forces.

General Stand Watie was greatly respected as a daring military master and strategist by the Union generals. In 1864, Watie was in command of the Indian Cavalry Brigade.

The brigade was composed of the First and Second Cherokee Cavalry, the Creek Squadron, the Osage Battalion, and the Seminole Battalion. Headquartered south of the Canadian River, Watie sent squads to raid and plunder the federal details around Fort Gibson. On June 10, 1864, his forces captured the stern-wheeler, "J.P. Williams," which was laden with supplies and goods worth approximately 1.5 million dollars. He was promoted to brigadier general. On September 19, 1864, his forces were victorious at the second battle of Cabin Creek. General Stand Watie was the last Confederate general to surrender after the Civil War. He surrendered at Doaksville, Indian Territory, on June 23, 1865.

Stand Watie circa 1855

The Civil War

By the onset of the Civil War, the Old Settlers and the Immigrants had been involved in their own Civil War. There was a great deal of animosity on the part of the Old Settlers toward the Immigrants for pushing them out of the government and basically ostracizing them. The two groups formed companies that joined in the fighting along side either the Union or the Confederate States in the war. One such group, commanded by Stand Watie, destroyed the home of Chief John Ross at Parkhill, Oklahoma.

The Civil War was bitterly contested among the Native Americans in Oklahoma. For the Cherokee, it was a war of brother against brother. Three thousand Cherokee enlisted in the Confederate Army while 1,000 Old Settlers fought for the Union. Cherokee Civil War units included: First Cherokee Mounted Rifles; First Arkansas Cherokee; First Cherokee Mounted Volunteers; Watie's Regiment, the Cherokee Mounted Volunteers; Second Regiment Cherokee Mounted Rifles of Arkansas; First Regiment Cherokee Mounted Riflemen; First Squadron Cherokee Mounted Volunteers; Second Cherokee Mounted Volunteers; Second Regiment Cherokee Mounted Rifles or Riflemen, and Cherokee Regiment.

Cherokee units fought at Wilson Creek (1861) and Pea Ridge (1862). There were few large battles in Oklahoma, but these were brutal. In November of 1861, a combined force of 1,400 Cherokee, Chickasaw, Choctaw, and Texas cavalry commanded by Colonel Douglas Cooper attacked a refugee column of 4,000 pro-Union Creek trying to reach safety in Kansas. Over 700 refugees were killed during the three day battle before reason took hold. After two assaults against the Creek, the Cherokee refused to participate in a third and withdrew. Meanwhile, the Cherokee allegiance to the Confederacy faltered. Following the Confederate defeat at Pea Ridge, John Ross switched sides to the Union. Actually, Ross allowed his capture in 1862 and spent the rest of the war in Philadelphia. John Drew's Mounted Rifle Regiment deserted and was reorganized as a regiment in the Union army, but other Cherokee units under Stand Watie remained loyal to the Confederacy.

The fighting in Oklahoma degenerated into the same vicious guerilla warfare that prevailed among the white settlers of Kansas and Missouri. Stand Watie, who became a Confederate general, was a leader of the Treaty Party and personally hated John Ross. After Ross switched allegiance in 1862 and went east, Stand Watie was elected Principal Chief of the Cherokee Nation in August. He captured the Cherokee capitol at Tahlequah and ordered Ross's home burned. The fighting produced hatreds that, added to the earlier differences, endured long after the war was over. Many Oklahoma Indians fled north to escape the fighting. Kansas eventually had more than 7,000 refugees from the Indian Territory which it could not house or feed. Many froze to death or starved. Heavily involved in the fighting throughout the war, the Cherokee Nation lost more than 1/3 of its population. No state, north or south, even came close to this. On June 23, 1865, Stand Watie was the last Confederate general to surrender his command to the United States.

Afterwards, the victorious federal government remembered the services of General Stand Watie to the Confederacy. It also remembered the 1861 vote by the Cherokee legislature to secede from the United States. These provided the excuse to invalidate all previous treaties between the Cherokee and United States. Therefore, the government sought to force the sale of over seven million acres of land in Oklahoma, Arkansas, Missouri, and Kansas by violation of treaty and international law. The U.S. sold the land of the Western Cherokee repeatedly until they finally sold it to white settlers. The United States ignored the sovereignty of the Western Cherokee Nation of Arkansas and Missouri and recognized John Ross as the leader of the Cherokee in Indian Territory. The Eastern Cherokee were settled on Western Cherokee land and the Western Cherokee were reduced to a minority on their own sovereign land.

John Ross died in 1866, and in new treaties imposed in 1866 and 1868, large sections of Cherokee lands were taken for railroad construction, white settlement (1889), or the relocation of other tribes. The Cherokee Nation never recovered to the prosperity it had enjoyed before the Civil War. As railroads were built across Cherokee lands, outlaws discovered that the Indian Territory, especially the Cherokee Nation, was a sanctuary from federal and state laws. Impoverished by the war, the Cherokee also began to lease lands to white tenant farmers. By 1880, whites outnumbered the Indians in the Indian Territory.[iii]

Stand Watie

After the Civil War

Following the Civil War, the government again began to take land from our forefathers and give it to white men. As far as the Old Settlers or Western Cherokee are concerned, there is little information available with the exception of a few court records of suits brought by the Old Settlers against the United States concerning the Treaties of 1817, 1819, 1828, and finally, the Treaty of 1846. See the excerpts following:

[iv]UNITED STATES v. 'OLD SETTLERS.'
'OLD SETTLERS' v. UNITED STATES.
Nos. 1,031 and 1,032.

Supreme Court of the United States

April 3, 1893.

Appeals from the Court of Claims

Petition by Bryan, Wilson, and Hendricks, under Act. Feb. 25, 1889, (25 St. at Large, p. 694,) for themselves, and as commissioners of the 'Old Settlers,' or 'Western Cherokee,' Indians, to recover moneys alleged to be due from the United States. A decree was given for petitioners. Both parties appeal. Modified and affirmed.

Statement by Mr. Chief Justice Fuller:

The original petition was filed March 8, 1889, and the substituted petition, January 23, 1890, and thereby the petitioners, Bryan, Wilson, and Hendricks, purporting to act for themselves and as the commissioners of the "Old Settlers," or*428 "Western Cherokee," Indians, represented that the latter are that part of the Cherokee race of Indians which formerly composed the Western Cherokee Nation, and which subsequently became known as the 'Old Settlers,' and that for the purpose of prosecuting their claims against the United States government they had appointed Bryan, Wilson, and Hendricks as their commissioners to represent and in their names and for their benefit to do and perform any and all acts and things necessary and proper to be done by them in the premises. That the suit was brought under the provisions of the act of congress approved February 25, 1889, entitled 'An act to authorize the court of claims to hear, determine, and render final judgment upon the claim of the Old Settlers, or Western Cherokee Indians,' ... It was further averred that, according to the foregoing itemized statement under article 4 of the treaty of 1846, their account with the United States should be stated as follows:

By "treaty fund," under 4th article, treaty 1846		$5,600,000 00
To improvements	$1,540,572 27	
" ferries	159,572 12	
" spoliations	264,894 09	
" additional lands	500,000 00	
" invested funds	500,000 00	
" removal, 2,200 Indians	44,000 00	
	$3,009,038 48	$5,600,000 70
		(3,009,038 48)
Balance of "treaty fund," after proper reductions		$2,590,961 52

By one third of the above balance, under terms of said 4th article of treaty of 1846... $863,653 84

To appropriation, Act Sept. 30, 1850.............. 532,896 96

"Principal sum due under 4th article of Treaty of 1846 .... $330,756 94

By value of lands		$5,671,164. 72 ½
"Property destroyed, etc....	30,000. 00	
" value of lands and improvements in Arkansas	9,179 .16 1/4	
To one third price additional lands	$166,666. 66 2/3	
"One third permanent investment fund	166,666 .66 2/3	
"Payment, act of September 30, 1850	532,896. 90	
	$866,230 .23 1/3	$5,710,343 .88 3/4
		(866,230 .23 1/3)
Balance...........		$4,844,113. 65

'For this amount, together with interest at the rate of 5 per centum per annum from June 12, 1838, until paid, your petitioners ask for a decree.'

(The officer thus referred to was Judge Parris of Maine, and the record contains the report of the second comptroller and second auditor of the treasury giving a statement of the account of the Cherokee Nation of Indians according to the principles established by the treaty. The items of charges against the Cherokee nation are given in detail and deducted from $6,647,067, the amount specified in article 9 of the treaty, being made up of the $5,000,000, the $600,000, and the $1,047,067.)

The account as stated in the Senate report was as follows:

This fund, provided by the treaty of 1835, consisted of

$5, 600, 000.

From which are to be deducted, under the treaty of 1846,

(4th article,) the sums
chargeable under the 15th article of the
treaty of 1835, which, according to the
report of the accounting officers, will stand thus:

For improvements	$1,540,572 27
For ferries	159,572 12
For spoliations......................	264,894 09

For removal and subsistence
of 18,026 Indians, at $53.33 1/3
per head .... 961,386.68 *(This was paid to John Ross.)*

Debts and claims upon the
Cherokee Nation, viz.:
National debts
(10th article) $18,062 06
Claims of United States citizens

(10th article)	61,073 49
Cherokee committee (12th article)	22,212 76
----------	101,348 31

Amount allowed United States for additional quantity of land ceded...........	500,000 00
Amount invested as a general fund of the nation.......	500,880 00

Making in the aggregate the sum of....... 4,028,653.45

Which, being deducted from the treaty fund of $5,600,000,

Leaves the residuum, contemplated by the 4th article of the

Treaty of 1846, of $1,571,346.55

--**451** Of which amount one third was to be allowed to the Western Cherokees for their interest in the Cherokee country east, being the sum of $523,782.18, and an appropriation of that amount was recommended. The committee also considered the two questions referred to the senate in respect of whether the amount expended for subsistence should be borne by the United States or by the Cherokee funds; and whether the Cherokees should receive interest on the sums found due them from a misapplication of their funds; and recommended the adoption of the following resolutions, which were accordingly adopted, September 5, 1850, by the senate, as umpire, under article 11 of the treaty of 1846, (Senate Jour. 1st Sess. 31st Cong. 601:)

We approve of this disposition of the matter as just and appropriate under the circumstances, and a competent exercise of judicial power. The court decides and pronounces the decree to be carried into effect as between the persons and parties who have brought the case before it for decision, and none the less so because it leaves the mere matter of distribution to be conducted in the manner and through the agencies pointed out in the treaty.

The result is that we concur substantially in the conclusions reached by the court of claims, whose laborious and painstaking examination of the case has been of great assistance in the investigation we have bestowed upon it; and in respect of the difference in the amount found we direct the decree to be modified so as to provide for the recovery of the defendants of the sum of $212,376.94 instead of the sum of $224,972.68, in full of the per capita fund provided by the fourth article of the treaty between the United States and the Western Cherokees, dated August 6, 1846, together with interest thereon at the rate of 5 per centum per annum from the 12th day of June, 1838, up to and until the modification of the decree, in addition to the sum of $4,179.26; and, as so modified, to be affirmed.

(Mr. Justice Jackson did not sit in this case or take part in its decision.)

This did not resolve the issues concerning our identity as a tribe; but it does give evidence that the U.S. government recognized us as a tribal entity in 1893.

The Dawes Commission

In 1885, a well intentioned, but ill-informed, Senator Henry Dawes of Massachusetts decided that holding of land in common was delaying the progress of Indians towards "civilization." Forming an alliance with western congressmen who wished to exploit Indian treaty lands, he secured passage of the General Allotment (Dawes) Act in 1887 that ultimately cost Native Americans 2/3 of their remaining land base. The Five Civilized Tribes of Oklahoma were exempt from allotment, but came under tremendous pressure to accept it. Until the 1880's, cattle from the Chisholm and Texas trails routinely grazed on the lands of the Cherokee Outlet before going to the Kansas railheads. The Cherokee earned a good income from this enterprise until the Commissioner of Indian Affairs halted it without explanation in 1890. It should also be noted that the Oklahoma Territory was organized that same year from the western half of the Indian Territory, and there may have been some connection! After the Cherokee were forced to sell, the land was made available for white settlement.

The Dawes Commission attempted to get the Five Tribes to accept allotment in 1893, but they refused. This led to the passage of the Curtis Act (1895) which dissolved tribal governments and forced allotment during 1901. Grafting of Indian lands became a massive and unofficially sanctioned form of theft in Oklahoma. Of the original seven million acres granted the Cherokee in the New Echota Treaty, the Cherokee Nation kept less than 1/3 of 1%. As compensation, the Cherokee became citizens in 1901 and were finally allowed to vote. An attempt by the Five Tribes to form their own state of Sequoyah in eastern Oklahoma failed in 1905, and the Cherokee Nation was officially dissolved on March 3, 1906. The following year, Oklahoma was admitted as the 46th state. The present government of the Cherokee Nation was formed in 1948 after passage of the Wheeler-Howard Indian Reorganization Act (1934). In 1961, the U.S. Claims Court awarded $15,000,000 to the Cherokee Nation for the lands of the Cherokee Outlet.[v] Rod Otter Johnson says, "The whole Dawes deal was sad. The government made it almost impossible for many to make the long trip to register. They had begun to be settled into farming. We know that farming then took more effort and time than it does now. My great great grandfather wanted to take his family to register from Arkansas, but they were afraid the crops would fail, or the whites would take their land just as they did in Georgia. This was told to me by my great grandfather. It seems that it was a very common concern."

ORIGINAL DAWES COMMISSION
H. L. DAWES, CAPT. A. S. McKENNON, M. H. KIDD

Western Cherokee Government

Sept. 11, 1824 - While in Arkansas, the Cherokee formally organized their government along democratic lines. Executive power was vested in a first, second and third chief. John Jolly was elected first chief, Black Coat was second chief, and Walter Webber was third chief. War with the Osage necessitated having three leaders.

Cherokee had a hunting area allotted to them known as Lovely's Purchase. The Osage considered it their hunting ground, too. This caused continual strife between the two tribes. Fort Gibson Military Post was established as a buffer zone in 1824 to protect these two tribes from one another.

Whites were settling Western Cherokee land, and this intrusion caused alarm. On December 28, 1827, the Cherokee appointed Black Fox, John Rogers, Thomas Graves, Thomas Maw, George Morris, Tobacco Will, and George Guess (Sequoyah) to go to Washington to protest this intrusion.

This delegation had no authority to allot land. However, they were forced to negotiate a treaty on May 6, 1828, whereby they gave up land in Arkansas for land in what is now Oklahoma. The Cherokee were given until July of 1829 to start moving, but many had to move early as settlers went into their homes and crowded them out.

The Move to Present Day Oklahoma

In 1828-29, Cherokee established settlements in Indian Territory (eastern Oklahoma). Jolly's home was about 3 miles east of present day Gore. His hewed log home had massive stone fireplace chimneys and large comfortable rooms. Other buildings served as homes for the servants who operated his large plantation that was well stocked with cattle. His home was always open to visitors of which he had many. It is reported that Jolly never slaughtered less than one beef a week throughout the year for his table.

Jolly's name was Oo-loo-te-ke meaning "He-Puts-the-Drum-Away." Wise, intelligent and affectionately called, "Beloved Father," he was a half-blood who spoke no English. Mixed bloods were considered full bloods if they spoke only Cherokee. He dressed, as did most Cherokee, in a hunting coat of cotton or wool, cloth leggings, beaded moccasins, and a cloth turban. His word was "inviolable, and his generosity knew no bounds, but the limitation of his means." Jolly died in December of 1838.

Sam Houston

In January, Houston married Eliza Allen, the daughter of an ex-governor. Elected in 1827, Houston resigned in 1829 as governor of Tennessee when his marriage ended. With no explanations, he left his state, wife, friends, and family for a three-year stay with the Western Cherokee.

Arriving aboard the steam ship Facility, runners reached Jolly with the news of the arrival of his adopted son, "The Raven." Notables of the nation were on hand to receive the distinguished visitor being escorted to the home of Jolly.

News reached all parts of the Nation. Citizens began arriving at Jolly's home. Among the guests were Big Canoe, Black Coat, Walter Webber, Little Terrapin, Young Elder, and Old Swimmer. No larger crowd of Cherokee ever gathered in what is now Sequoyah County than when Sam Houston arrived.

Houston established a home north of Fort Gibson and lived with his Cherokee wife, Tiana Rogers, daughter of John Rogers and niece of John Jolly. She shared "Wigwam Neosho" with Houston until he went to Texas.

Active in political affairs of the Nation, Houston was adopted as a tribal member by the Cherokee on October 31, 1831. Along with helping the Cherokee, the Creek and Osage sought his advice. He made trips to Washington in their behalf.

In Texas, Houston became Commander-in-Chief of American Forces and on April 21, 1836, defeated Santa Anna's force of 1800 soldiers. Upon establishing the Texas Republic, he was elected its first president. After Texas became a state, he was elected governor.

In the summer of 1829, Houston lay on a mat of corn shucks under the loving care of the Jolly household. In September, he wrote, "I am very feeble from a long spell of fever which... well nigh closed the scene of all my mortal cares, but I thank my God that I am again cheered by the hope of renewed health."

Sam Houston

Cherokee Capitol 1828-39

A capitol was established east of Jolly's home. The council house, grounds, and home of the first chief made up the national capitol called Tahlonteeskee in honor of the chief's brother. The general council met there to make laws from 1828-39.

The general council elected chiefs who served for 4 years. The first and second chief received $100 annually and the third chief $60. The general council consisted of two houses, the national committee and the council. These two bodies were made up of two representatives from the districts of the nation. Thus, there were eight members in each house. The general council convened in October and was divided into four districts: Sallisaw, Lee's Creek, Illinois, and Neosho.

District officials were judges and two Light Horse (sheriff) were elected by citizens for two years. District judges received an annual salary of $25, and the Light Horse received $40.

National Laws

The Chief approved any laws that were passed by the general council. Punishment was whipping or death, and penalties were decided by the judge and administered by the Light Horse. Crimes such as theft, rape, robbery, and breaking open or burning houses were punishable by 25 to 60 lashes on the bare back.

A person guilty of cutting down a pecan tree was fined five dollars. A portion of the fine went to the informer and a portion to the Light Horse. The same fine was inflicted on a person for setting woods on fire before the first of March.

Another law provided death for bargaining away land of the nation. If a person was found guilty of selling off land sections or other divisions, he received 100 lashes on the bare back.

Any citizen who harbored a criminal of the U.S. was to pay a fine of $100. This law was the first passed by any tribe in the state of Oklahoma. Dealing with the outlaw problem was a serious matter for the U.S. and Indian Territory. In 1832, schools were provided in each district and employed Sequoyah to supervise the teaching of his syllabary at $400 annually.

After the forced removal of the Eastern Cherokee in 1838-39, Tahlonteeskee was discontinued as capitol. For a short time the capitol was at Takatoka north of Tahlequah, but it was eventually moved to Tahlequah where it remains today. John Ross was the leader of the Eastern Cherokee, and he was elected principal chief under the protest of the Western Cherokee. He served in this position for approximately 40 years.

Tahlonteeskee continued as the Illinois District and a meeting place for Old Settlers. Meetings were held at Tahlonteeskee with the purpose of settling differences between the factions of the tribe. By 1846, there was a shaky unification of the three factions (Old Settlers, Treaty Party, and the Ross Party). The Cherokee Nation moved into what has been referred to as the "Golden Age." They became prosperous through their industry and cooperation. The outbreak of the Civil War ended this peaceful period as "battle lines" were once again drawn. John Ross wanted to remain neutral while others, mainly those who had signed the Treaty of New Echota and Old Settlers, wanted to fight for the Southern cause.

The reconstructed site of Tahlonteeskee, three miles east of Gore on HWY 64, has a council house and courthouse. There is a log cabin that belonged to the Carlile-Foreman family who were Old Settlers. On private property north of this site is the Tahlonteeskee remains. There are still signs of a foundation, an old well, and a little cemetery that is almost erased from sight. [vi]

Our Cherokee Spiritual Heritage

The Legend of the Keetoowah Cherokee

In 1930, Levi B. Gritts, a prominent member of the traditionalist Keetoowah Society, recalled "The Legend of the Keetoowah Cherokee" which placed them on islands in the Atlantic Ocean east of South America. Anthropologists have discovered that Cherokee basket and pottery styles resemble those of South American and Caribbean tribes. The styles and designs differ from other tribal designs of the southeast U.S.

Seventy tribes attacked them, but by the guidance of God, they were victorious. The last warrior of their attackers, Ner-du-er-gi, was on top of a mountain overlooking their camp in the deep valley below. This warrior saw a smoke arising from the camp that "extended up beyond Heaven." The smoke was divided into three parts that depicted an eagle holding arrows. When the warrior and his followers saw this, he ordered them not to attack the Indians for they were God's people and powerful. If they attacked, they would be destroyed.

When God created these people, he gave them great, mysterious power to be used for the best interests of the people. They then lived in large cities with tall buildings. Some wise men began to use their power differently than was intended. This troubled the people. God instructed them to take their white fire and move away from that place. Some went to Asia, some to India, and others to North America leaving the wise men behind. After they had gone to other countries, these large cities were destroyed when the ground sank. The large cities are now under the ocean. God turned to the people that came to America and gave them wisdom and guidance. There came a time when the people began to violate their teachings by committing crimes against each other, committing murders, and feuding between the seven clans. The people met with their medicine men around their fire to ask God for guidance. The medicine men were inspired to go up to a high mountain, one at a time, on each of seven days.

On the seventh day, they heard a noise over them and a light brighter than day appeared. A voice said, "I am a messenger from God. God has heard your prayers and He has great passion for your people and from now on you shall be called Keetoowah. Go back to your fire and worship. There is a white ball from way east who is your enemy coming, and your grandchildren's feet are directed west. They shall have great trials on the edge of the prairie. They shall be divided into different factions, and their blood shall be about only one-half. Families shall be divided against each other, and they shall disregard their chiefs, leaders, medicine men, and captains. But, if these younger generations should endeavor to follow your God's instruction, there is a chance to turn back east. If not, the next move shall be west and on to the coast. From there, they will go on to the boat, and this shall be the last."

Yowah the Creator

So, in the heart of the Smokey Mountains, some 3500 years ago, God revealed Himself to our people. The Creator gave our people a new name --- "Keetoowah." The town of Keetoowah was located near present day Bryson City, North Carolina. It was from Keetoowah that the Creator revealed His true name to us. He said His name was "Yowah" and His people would be "kit-Yowah" or "from God." Today, we are known as the Cherokee. At the advent of European contact, we, the Cherokee, had become the most powerful tribal group in the American southeast. We claimed parts of nine states. The colonists knew us as the most civilized tribe, because we chose to adopt many of the newcomer's ways. One of those ways was the belief in Jesus Christ as the Son of Yowah.

Theories in reference to the Cherokee and the lost tribes of Judah have arisen over the years, and there have been many investigations. The evidence, at best, was inconclusive. It was supposedly proven both yes and no, but the truth is that it is completely unprovable either way. James Adair, an Irish trader who lived among the Cherokee for 40 years, decided the Indians were indeed one of the lost tribes of Judah and wrote 70,000 words on the subject. He used as evidence such topics as their division into tribes; their language and dialects; their festivals, feasts, and religious rites; their absolutions and anointings; their laws of uncleanness; their avoidance of unclean things; the practices of marriage, divorce, and punishment for adultery, and their ornamentation.

Cherokees were often selected for distinction, because they were inheritors of a dignity beyond their rather simple means. They even referred to themselves as the "principal people." Their lands were the center of the Earth, and all else radiated out from there. ii

It's interesting to note the similarities of the names. Yowah, as God revealed Himself to the Cherokees, and Jehovah, as God revealed Himself to the Hebrews and Christians, are similar in context. The name for God in the Old Testament of the Bible is Jehovah. The Hebrew "Jehovah" was specifically pronounced "Yehova". Other similarities worthy of consideration have been noted in regard to rituals, laws, and sanctuary cities. Is the Cherokee Yowah the Biblical Jehovah? Did God reveal Himself to the Cherokee just as He did to the Hebrews? My belief is yes. The Bible says in Romans 1:19-20: " ... what may be known of God is manifest in them, for God has shown it to them. For since the creation of the world His invisible attributes are clearly seen, being understood by the things that are made, even His eternal power and Godhead, so that they are without excuse." NKJV   So, it stands to reason that God would reveal Himself to the Cherokee people as well. Because God is the same yesterday today and forever, and He never changes, then the laws that He would give the Cherokee would not differ much from the laws that He would give the Hebrews. This, in my opinion, negates any notion that the Cherokee somehow migrated from the Middle East to North America. The theory that Native Americans are descendents of the lost tribe of Judah is only a theory, and one that I, personally, do not accept especially in the light of Biblical evidence that God revealed Himself to of all mankind. We have seen this in the Biblical book of Romans. There is other evidence as well. The Bible speaks of God revealing Himself to others in the person of Jesus. For example in John 10:15-16, Jesus says, *"As the Father knows Me, even so I know the Father; and I lay down My life for the sheep. And other sheep I have which are not of this fold; them also I must bring, and they will hear My voice; and there will be one flock and one shepherd."* NKJV

Belief in one Supreme Being, Yowah, formed a central theme of Cherokee religion. His name was so sacred that certain priests could not speak it aloud. Even such individuals, dedicated from childhood to the performance of religious rites, uttered it in public only while singing a hymn that was sung but once a year.

Yowah was understood as the unity of three beings that were referred to as "the Elder Fires above." They were the creators of the universe. These Elder Fires first created the sun and the moon and gave the world its form. Then, they returned to the seventh heaven in the sky. They left the sun and the moon to finish the creation of the stars and all living things and to rule over them. This explains why Cherokee prayers used the expression, "Sun, my creator."

Cherokees and Christianity

Mainly influenced by the Baptists and Methodists, churches sprang up all over Cherokee country. One Baptist missionary and his Cherokee co-worker, who were especially sensitive to the Cherokee culture, started over 30 churches and trained several dozen Cherokee ministers.

The Cherokee have embraced Christianity, not because it was forced upon them, but because they have truly come to understand that Yowah, the Creator, had revealed Himself to others as well.

There are many legends among Native Americans of a man from the East who walked the lands teaching peace and love and care for the Earth. He is known by many names, but many Cherokee Christians believed His name was Jesus.

Many atrocities were committed in the name of Christianity against Native Americans. These were very wrong and truly not Biblical. Most true Christians today, whether white or red, truly grieve that these things were done by evil men in God's name. However, if one studies the history of the Cherokee, you will begin to understand that the Cherokee actually invited the Christians into their lands to establish schools and teach them, not only academics, but biblical principles as well. Men such as Major Ridge, a prominent Cherokee leader, were enthusiastic about bringing in the Christian schools to Cherokee country. His family became Christian; though, he himself resisted until late in life. The Christian schools brought much in the way of education and improvement of life to Cherokee people. Most importantly, it brought to them a saving knowledge of Jesus Christ.

If one did a survey today of the Western Cherokee Old Settlers, he would find that the majority, perhaps approaching 90%, are Christian. How can we reconcile our Christian heritage and our Cherokee heritage in spirituality and traditional ceremonies?

Many of the old stories that we hear, some of which are included here in this book, are allegorical in nature.

They symbolize in physical imagery a spiritual truth. Many of these old stories were intended for children.

The ceremonies of the Cherokee are to honor the Great Spirit, Yowah, and His spirit helpers. In Christianity, we have ceremonies that honor our God and recognize His interaction with us. For the Cherokee, their purpose and mission in life is to care for God's creation. For the Christian, their purpose in life is to have a personal relationship with God through Jesus Christ. A perfect blending of these two cultures would give us the purpose of having a personal relationship with God through Jesus Christ. We care for His creation. This is evident if one reads in Genesis 2:15 where it says *"...then the Lord God took the man and put him in the Garden of Eden to attend and keep it."* As we look at some of these ceremonies of the Cherokee, we will look for, and identify, elements that reflect that purpose for all of God's people.

"Yowah" keeper of the fire

Ceremonies and Traditions of the Cherokee

(From Elder Ben Little Hawk Stephens)

Wapani (Give Away)

The general purpose of the Give Away (Wapani) is to devalue the material aspects of life, while at the same time exalting the spiritual values of giving. The objective of the Wapani is to give something away. You may give to anyone including someone you don't know, a relative, or a friend. Perhaps, you will experience the highest form of Give Away, which is forgiveness. Forgive an enemy or a foe. Maybe, you will Give Away love to someone that you consider unlovable.

In a material sense, you may Give Away something that means quite a bit to you. Perhaps, you will Give Away something you made yourself with a special blessing. Perhaps, you will Give Away something in your medicine pack. Whatever you Give Away, it must be meaningful to you. To Give Away in a sacred manner, you must Give Away thoughtfully and with caring. If you Give Away a light that was used in a sacred manner, make sure that it has been "smudged." This will cleanse it of any possible misuse or handling by an unclean person before you hand it on to another.

The person receiving your Wapani need not know the significance of the gift. You should not demand thanks or appreciation. To Give Away is the purpose, not thanks for the thing given. In your meditations for a few days after practicing Wapani, be alert to recognize the effects this Give Away has had upon you and your progress on the medicine path. The Give Away must not be practiced once and then forgotten. You should Give Away to mark all special milestones upon your path.

It is not wrong to possess material items. Excessive attachment to these material things will impede your progress on the medicine path. Above all, remember to give your love to every living thing. We are all related, and the love will come back to you.

Luke 6:38 *"....give, and it will be given to you: good measure, pressed down, shaken together, and running over will be put into your bosom. For with the same measure that you use, it will be measured back to you."*

Smudging

Smudging is very similar in purpose to the Christian practice of anointing with oil. Various Christian congregations utilize the anointing oil in different ways. A number of these ways coincide with smudging. Keep in mind that this is ceremonial and not sacramental in nature.

You will need the following items in order to smudge:

Herbs: Sage, sweet grass, cedar, tobacco, or other herbs singly or in combination

Container: A shell or a natural-made bowl (clay, pottery)

Other: A feather or fan, matches, sand or fine soil.

The estimated time involved is five minutes, if you are alone. If you are with a group, more time will be required. Following is the procedure for smudging individuals and an area where a meeting or Pow Wow is to take place.

1. Mix together the herbs you will be using. Place them in a shell or natural-made starting bowl and light them. Since some mixtures of the herbs do not burn well, you may need to put a piece of charcoal in the bowl first. Before lighting either the charcoal or herbs, make sure there is some soil or sand in the bottom of the bowl or shell. This will keep the container from being too hot to hold.

2. When the herbs are burning, use a fan or a feather from a domestically raised bird (*chicken, turkey, pheasant, or duck) to fan the flame outward. Throughout the ceremony, you will need to fan the herbs to keep them smoldering. (*Non-Indians are not permitted to possess eagle feathers.)

3. Once the herbs are smoldering, purify any medicine tools you are using by passing them through the smoke. Use the feather to fan the smoke (not the bowl, just the smoke) to your heart, in over your head, down your arms, and down the front of your body. Next, move the smoke over the back of your body toward the ground. If you need special balancing or healing in some part of your body, you can emphasize by pulling the smoke to that area.

4. Purify the area by using the feather to waft smoke from the container. If you are inside, smudge around the walls of the room paying particular attention to the corners of the room.

5. Offer smoke to the six directions: up to the Creator, down to the Earth, and then to the North, East, South, and West in that order.

6. For the individual ceremony, use the feather to draw the smoke to the person's heart, in over their head, down their arms, and down to the front of their body. Move the smoke over the back of the person's body toward the ground. If special balancing or healing is needed in some part of the body, pull the smoke to that area.

7. Purify the area by using the feather to waft smoke from the container. If you are inside, smudge around the walls of the room paying particular attention to the corners of the room.

The Sacred Fire

To make sacred fires, clan representatives gathered wood from the eastern sides of seven trees, peeled off the outer bark, and placed the wood in a circle on the central altar of the town house. These woods included: white oak, black oak, water oak, black jack, basswood, chestnut, and white pine. Once the fire ignited, women carried burning coals to start fresh fires in their homes. The town house fire never went out. It burned continuously in each town house until it was ceremonially extinguished and rebuilt. Neither embers nor ash could be removed from the fire. No pipes could be lit there. Cherokee offered supplication through the fire whose smoke was always in readiness to convey the petition on high. The fire was the source of heat, light, and smoke that rose from the town house to the Upper World. Wood for the townhouse fire carried singular significance.

Purification

Purification does not come from the A'si (the hothouse). For our people, purification comes from the river (the Yunwi Gunahita---Long Man). Our people would wade out into the river facing the rising sun and while reciting prayers, dip seven times under the water. This was done every morning, no matter how cold the water. (This is known as "going to water".) Water is a sacred messenger to Unequa. There are two forms of "going to water."

One form is called Amayi Ditatiyi (taking them to water) in which the water was simply dipped up with the hand and spread over the person's head and body.

The second form is called Atawastiyi in which the person plunged or went entirely under the surface of the water. The person "going to water" faced east and dipped himself under the water, or dipped water over himself, seven times.

The A'si is sometimes mistaken for the Plains Indian's "Sweat Lodge", but the A'si was used mainly for the purpose of healing. When someone was sick or ill, they would strip and enter the A'si. Rocks would be placed in the center and heated. Then, a mixture made of the beaten root of the wild parsnip would be poured over the rocks. Today, it is water that is used. The use of wild parsnip is not practiced anymore. The ill person would remain in the A'si until they were in a profuse sweat and choking on the fumes. They would then leave the A'si and go to a nearby stream where they would leap into the water.

Pow Wow Protocol

When you attend a Pow Wow, it is important to remember that you are a guest and an observer of ancient ceremonies and traditions that have survived every possible adversity. Here are things you need to know for proper behavior:

1. Under no circumstances are alcohol or drugs allowed on Pow Wow grounds. Alcohol is the greatest curse ever visited on the Native American, and it will not be tolerated. If you come to a Pow Wow drunk, or bring alcohol or drugs with you, you will be escorted out by tribal security. If you can't stay sober for a few hours, then you're in the wrong place.

2. The area for dancing and ceremonies is called the Arena, and hay bales set in a circle usually mark its boundaries. There is a sheltered area that can either be in the form of an arbor or canopy that designates a resting place for the Elders, the dancers, singers, and the Pow Wow officials. Take care not to sit in these places. They are easy to spot if you pay attention. There will be chairs, articles of clothing, and other personal belongings in plain sight. If you see blankets laid out on hay bales, do not sit there, as they are reserved for the owner of the blanket. Please be respectful for that person or family.

3. It is common to see teepees and lodges set up on the grounds. These are not open to the public. Pow Wow participants live in the teepees during the gathering. In fact, the teepees are their homes for the duration. Respect their privacy. Teepees and other structures set up for classes and demonstrations will be clearly marked. If a map or guide to the area is offered, it would be a good idea to get one.

4. Once the dance Arena has been blessed with sage and prayer, it becomes spiritual ground. Do not walk across the Arena, and don't allow your children to run into the Arena. The announcer or other Pow Wow official will chastise you. There is no safer place for children than a Pow Wow, but that should not be a signal for them to run wild and be disrespectful.

5. Don't take pictures at random---neither still shots nor video. Some large Pow Wows require that you register your camera and will place a number on it. The announcer will tell the audience when pictures are permitted. Pay attention. Cameras have been confiscated and film destroyed, because people did not listen and did not take instructions seriously. If there is a particular dance you want to photograph, ask permission of the announcer. If he says no, give it up. Some dances are sacred and are never to be photographed. If you see a dancer who is especially striking, ask if you may take a picture after he or she leaves the arena. It would be a courtesy to take his or her name and address and send a print of the photo. Human kindness and consideration are always long remembered and deeply appreciated. Protocol for pictures varies depending upon the part of the country your visiting and the customs of the Pow Wow committee. If you see videos being filmed and professional looking camera crews, chances are they're representing a native organization that sells Pow Wow videos. Prior to the event, newspaper and magazine photographers have to get permission to film and take pictures. Be wise, and be cautious by asking first.

6. A dancer's clothing is Regalia. It is not a costume and is a prized possession. Some regalia have been handed down through the generations and are priceless. When a dancer decides to "come out" in a particular style, the regalia reflect the spirit and customs of the people being honored. This is no small decision, and a "coming out" ceremony for a new dancer is cause for great celebration. The regalia are usually handmade by the dancer, friends, and/or family. Every article has special meaning. It takes years to collect items to complete the regalia. This involves no small expense. Do not ever touch a dancer's regalia without permission. The regalia are an expression of spirit and has been prayed over and blessed. Honor it, the person wearing it, and the living history it represents.

7. Finally, put aside the Hollywood image of what an "Indian" looks like. Native Americans come in all sizes, shapes, and colors. From the milky skinned blue-eyed blonde, to the green-eyed redhead, or to the dark brown and black haired, they are all natives in their heritage, blood, and heart. Some are tall and stately; some are short and stocky. Some have long angular faces; some have round faces. Some have round eyes; some have almond shaped eyes. Some even have a definite oriental slant to their eyes. As you learn and become more knowledgeable of native history and anthropology, you will become aware that these physical characteristics are a clear indication of the lineage of that person's heritage. Do not be insensitive. Do not inquire as to whether someone is "Indian." Do not say, "How much Indian are you, anyway?"

Look, learn, and enjoy the Pow Wow!

Cherokee Herbs and Medicinal Remedies

Cherokee medicine is based on a spiritual and medical system carefully developed for more than 4,000 years and known as Nv wo ti. Cherokee herbalist use Nv wo ti to communicate with plants (Green People) asking for nourishment and guidance. Cherokee people believe that the Green People can treat ailments such as a cough. This helps the patient to connect with the Earth, or the Great Life, restoring balance and health.

Cold remedies

Wild cherry is a natural expectorant that will calm a cough and is safe even for children. Harvest the bark of wild cherry in the summer months, boil the bark until the water reaches a syrupy consistency, and administer the juice three times a day as needed. Wild cherry may be used to soothe a cough due to any type of illness including coughs caused by lung congestion.

To make a tea from the inner bark of white pine, pour 1 cup of boiling water over one tablespoon of the bark and drink the tea at least three times a day. Cherokee medicine uses white pine tea to treat a cough due to the common cold, flu, and bronchitis. A natural expectorant, white pine bark increases circulation helping the immune system to repel the viruses and phlegm that cause a cough.

Drink sarsaparilla. Add 3g of powdered sarsaparilla to juice three times a day. Drink daily until the cough subsides. Sarsaparilla is a common Cherokee medicine used to treat a variety of ailments. It is used for a cough. Its anti-inflammatory and stimulating properties soothe the lungs while helping to expel phlegm.

Take herbal supplements if tea and juice treatments aren't for you. Sarsaparilla and white pine are available in tincture and capsule form and can be found in most health food stores. Follow the manufacturer's directions for proper dosage information.

The following are cures for common ailments and weather predictors passed down to Annette Welch by her grandmother.

Diarrhea---Cover blackberries with water and simmer. Strain and drink the liquid to stop diarrhea.

Colic---Boil catnip in water, strain, and drink.

Earache---Catch a Betsy Bug and squeeze it in the ear.

Earache---Blow pipe smoke into the ear.

Ringworm---Slice the hull of a green black walnut and rub on the ringworm several times a day. The iodine in the walnut hull kills the ringworm.

Worms---Once a month, eat one peeled clove of garlic. This will worm both people and animals.

Toothache and Sore Throat---Cut small twigs off the Prickly Ash. Chew to relieve toothaches and sore throat.

Stomach Problems---Dig cattail roots, wash well, and simmer with a small amount of water. Eat like you would potatoes. This soothes an irritated stomach and is easy to digest.

Flu or Chest Colds---Simmer wild sage leaves in water. Strain and drink the tea. This also calms a sour stomach.

Kidney Problems---Dandelions were boiled, strained, and drunk for bladder and kidney problems.

Burns---Apply honey to the burned area.

Insect Sting and Bites---Coat the area with mud.

Constipation---Eat 3 or 4 persimmons daily to relieve constipation. They can be dried in the fall and used all year.

Cough---Sip a mixture of honey and water.

Skin Conditions---Eat cooked dock.

Body Purification---Dig sassafras roots, wash well, cut in chunks, cover with water, and boil for 1 hour. Set aside for 1 hour, strain, and cool. Adults drink 1 cup per day for three days. Children drink ½ cup per day for three days. This will purify the blood and build your body's defense against illness.

Liniment---This liniment has been used in our family for well over 100 years. The recipe was changed about 100 years ago to utilize easily obtainable, store-bought ingredients.
The prepared mixture will keep indefinitely and should be stored in a glass jar.

1 bottle Spirits of Camphor (2 fluid ounce container)
(Pour camphor into a quart jar. Use the camphor bottle to measure the other liquids before adding to the jar.)
2 ounces kerosene
2 ounces of turpentine
2 raw egg whites
Shake or mix well. Swab on cuts, abrasions, carbuncles, boils, insect bites, aches, and bruises on both man and beast. It smells terrible, but it works!

Persimmon Seed Weather Prediction

Every year my grandparents and parents would gather three persimmons to cut to predict the weather. (My family still does this every year in the fall. So far, it has been right on the mark.) You cut the flesh off the persimmon seeds. Choose one seed from each of three persimmons. Using a sharp knife, cut the seeds open and use the half-seed revealed to predict the weather. You can actually see a knife, fork, or spoon in the center of the seeds. We always cut three seeds, but they will all be alike depending on which area of the country in which you live. Here are the predictions.

Knife-----This means the winter will be extremely cold and possibly icy with little snow. The wind will "cut through you like a knife."

Spoon-----The spoon represents a snow shovel. The winter will have a lot of snow.

Fork-----The fork represents a mild winter with no extreme, or little extreme, weather.

Wooly Caterpillar and Squirrel Tail Weather Predictors

A wooly worm caterpillar has tiny black and orange hairs all over the top of its body. When there is more black than orange, get ready for a severe winter. When there is more orange than black hairs, you can look forward to a mild winter.

Check the squirrel's tails in the early fall. If the tails are extremely dense and bushy, get ready for a severe winter. If the tails are thinner and not as bushy, you can look forward to a mild winter. Also, squirrels will bury their horde of nuts deeper when the winter is going to be severe.

Tree Moss Weather Predictor

The more moss on the south side of a tree, the more severe the winter.

Snow

If snow lies on the ground for three days, it will snow again that winter. (I've been observing this for years. It is accurate.)

Some Plants and Herbs Commonly Used

Blackberry

One of the herbs known for years for soothing stomach problems is the blackberry. Using a strong tea from the roots is helpful in reducing and soothing swollen tissues and joints. An infusion from the leaves is also used as a tonic for stimulating the entire system. A decoction from the roots, sweetened with sugar or honey, makes syrup used as an expectorant. It is also healing for sore throats and gums. The leaves can also be chewed fresh to soothe bleeding gums. The Cherokee historically used the tea for curing diarrhea.

Gum (Black Gum)

Cherokee healers use a mild tea made from small pieces of the bark and twigs to relieve chest pains.

Hummingbird Blossoms (Buck Brush)

This herb is used by Cherokee healers who make a weak decoction of the roots for a diuretic that stimulates kidney function.

Cat Tail (Cattail Reed)

This plant is not a healing agent, but is used as preventative medicine. It is a bland, easily digestible food helpful for recovering from illness. Most all parts of the plant, except for the mature leaves and the seed head, are edible. Due to wide-spread growing areas, it is a reliable food source all across America. The root has a very high content of starch and can be gathered at any time. Preparation is very similar to potatoes and can be mashed, boiled, or even mixed with other foods. The male plant provides pollen that is a wonderful source of protein. It can be added as a supplement to other kinds of flour when making breads.

Pull Out a Sticker (Greenbriar)

A decoction of the small roots of this plant is useful as a blood purifier. It is also a mild diuretic. Some healers make a salve from the leaves and bark mixed with hog lard and apply it to minor sores, scalds, and burns. Some Cherokee healers also use the root tea for arthritis.

Mint

Mint teas are a stimulant for the stomach and an aid in digestion. The crushed and bruised leaves can be used as a cold compress, made into a salve, or added to the bath water, which relieves itching skin. Cherokee healers also use an infusion of the leaves and stems to lower high blood pressure.

Tobacco-like Plant (Mullein)

This is one of the oldest herbs, and some healers recommend inhaling the smoke from smoldering mullein roots and leaves to soothe asthma attacks and chest congestion. The roots can be made into a warm decoction for soaking swollen feet or reducing swelling in joints. It reduces swelling from inflammation and soothes painful, irritated tissue. It is particularly useful to the mucus membranes. A tea can be made from the flowers as a mild sedative.

Qua lo ga (Sumac)

All parts of the common sumac have a medicinal use. Mild decoctions from the bark can be used as a gargle for sore throats and may be taken as a remedy for diarrhea. A tea from the leaves and berries reduces fevers. Fresh bruised leaves and ripe berries are made into a poultice which soothes poison ivy. A drink from the ripened or dried berries makes a pleasant beverage which is a good source of vitamin C.

Squirrel Tail, or Saloli gatoga (Yarrow)

Yarrow has many uses. The best known use is to stop excessive bleeding. Freshly crushed leaves can be applied to open wounds or cuts and the properties of the herb will cause the blood to clot. A fresh juice of yarrow, diluted with spring or distilled water, can heal internal bleeding such as stomach and intestinal disorders. The leaves, prepared as a tea, are believed to stimulate intestinal functions and aid in digestion. It also helps the flow of the kidneys, as well as the gallbladder. A decoction made of the leaves and stems acts as an astringent and is a wonderful wash for all kinds of skin problems such as acne, chapped hands, and other irritations.

Looks Like Coffee, or Kawi Iyusdi (Yellow Dock)

This plant is not only a medicinal herb, but it also is a food. It is much like spinach, but believe it or not, contains more vitamins and minerals. Because of the long taproot, it gathers nutrients from deep underground. The leaves are a source of iron and also have laxative properties. Juices from the stems, prepared in a decoction, can be made into an ointment with beeswax and olive oil and used for itching, minor sores, diaper rash, and other irritations. Cherokee herbalists prescribe a warm wash made from the decoction of crushed roots for a disinfectant. Juice from the root, not prepared in any special way, is said to be a cure for ringworm.

Big Stretch or Nuyigala dinadanesgi utana (Wild Ginger)

The Cherokee commonly recommend a mild tea of this herb made from the rootstock, which is a mild stimulant for the digestive system. It can also help colic, intestinal gas, or the common upset stomach. A strong, hot infusion of the roots can act as an expectorant in eliminating mucus from the lungs. Fresh wild ginger may be substituted for the regular store-bought ginger root as a spice for cooking.

What Rabbits Eat, or Jisdu unigisdi (Wild Rose)

The ripe fruit of the wild rose is a rich source of Vitamin C and is a reliable preventative and curative for the common cold. The tea from the hips is a mild diuretic and stimulates the bladder and kidneys. When the infusion of the petals is used, it is an ancient remedy for sore throats. Cherokee healers recommend a decoction of the roots for diarrhea.

Willow Bark

The bark of the branches is stripped and dried. A tea is made from the bark that is useful for aches, pains, and headaches. This is the original aspirin!

Alfalfa

Alfalfa is full of calcium, vitamins A, B1, B6, B12, C, E, and niacin. It is very good for lowering cholesterol, preventing atherosclerosis, and for fighting infection.

Aloe Vera

The juice from the leaf of the aloe is a great remedy for minor burns and scratches. It also relieves warts, and of course, since it is composed of about 96% water, it also makes an excellent moisturizer.

Balm

Balm is known as lemon balm. When mixed with honey, it makes a good sipping tea and soothes sore, scratchy throats. You can also chop the leaves and place some into a cup of boiling water and drink as a balm tea, or add it to your own tea. It is very calming.

Cabbage

Cabbage is a good preventative for colon cancer as it contains histidine. Also, it helps keep low-density lipoproteins (bad cholesterol) out of the system. Raw cabbage juice is a good way to clean the digestive system.

Carrot

There is a natural antiseptic in a carrot that is effective in the mouth, and the juice can help skin swelling and inflammation. It lowers cholesterol and the beta-carotene in carrots is known to help fight cancer. And, of course, we all know that eating carrots somehow keeps the vision sharp.

Dandelion

Dandelions are good in salads, but the head should be collected before the plant flowers to add to the salad greens. There are lots of nutrients in dandelions.

Sage

Sage is considered sacred by many tribes. Sage leaves used as a tea are good for sore throat and congestion. It also helps out with bowel problems. You could make tea by adding 2 teaspoons of fresh or dried leaves to 2 cups of boiling water and steep. When feeling congested, hold a bundle of sage to your nose and inhale deeply. This will provide about four or five hours free breathing.

SAGE

Cherokee Foods and Recipes[vii]

Bean Bread
Tu-ya ga-du

- 1 cup of cornmeal
- ½ cup flour
- 2 tsp. baking powder
- 1 tbsp. sugar
- 2 cups milk
- ¼ cup melted shortening
- 1 beaten egg
- 2 tbsp. honey
- 4 cups drained brown beans

Set beans aside and mix all other ingredients. Fold beans into the mixture. Pour into a greased, heated pan. Bake at 450*F until browned. (Usually 30 minutes or so)

According to Aggie Lossiah, this is the old traditional recipe:

"Sure, corn meal is the main part of bean bread. Corn meal is the main part of the food eaten by us Indians. Beans are used, too. First, pour some water into this iron pot here over the fire. Sift in some good wood ashes. Pour in the shelled corn. Stir once in a while and let cook until the bubbles begin to come up. Take out a grain to test with the fingers to see if the skin is ready to slip. That is the way we tell if it has been in the lye water long enough. Wash the corn in a basket sieve to get rid of the skins. Put the corn into the wooden beater (Ka No Na) and beat it with a heavy piece of wood. Yes, use the little end; the big end is to give weight. Feel the meal to see if it is fine enough. The hot beans and their soup are poured into the pan of meal. No, leave out the salt. Work quickly so the mixture will not get cold. Work the mixture into a ball. Flatten the ball because we are making "broadswords" as my granddaddy called them. Wrap the corn blades around the dumpling. (The blades were pulled green and hung up by the little end to dry, then scalded to make limber.) Fold the ends under to hold, or tie with a strong grass. We'll cook these in the iron pot out by the branch. The clear water I left out there should be boiling by now. The bean dumplings will have to boil about an hour." (To prevent crumbling, do not put any salt into Bean Bread.)

Fried Hominy

- 2 strips of good bacon
- 2 cups of hominy
- 2 or 3 green onions

Fry bacon while cutting green onions into small pieces. Crumble bacon and add onions. When the onions begin to fry, add hominy and cook for about 10 to 15 minutes. Begin cooking on high heat, and lower heat as it cooks.

Grape Dumplings

- 1 cup flour
- 1 ½ tsp. baking powder
- 2 tsp. sugar
- ¼ tsp. salt

- 1 tbsp. shortening
- ½ cup grape juice

Mix flour, baking powder, sugar, salt, and shortening. Add juice and mix into a stiff dough. Roll the dough very thin on a floured board and cut into strips ½" wide. (You can roll dough in your hands and break into pea-sized bits.) Drop into boiling grape juice and cook for 10 - 12 minutes.

Cherokee Bread Pudding

- 2 1/2 cups toasted bread cubes
- 2 1/2 cups scalded milk
- 1 cup butter
- 1/2 cup sorghum
- pinch of salt
- 2 eggs, beaten
- 1 tablespoon pure maple syrup

Preheat oven to 350°F. Lightly grease a casserole dish. Pour scalded milk over bread and let stand 5 minutes. Heat sorghum, butter, and salt in a saucepan. Gradually pour over bread mixture. Cool. Gradually pour mixture over eggs. Stir in maple syrup. Pour into casserole dish. Place dish in a pan of hot water and bake in oven for 50-60 minutes or until firm.

Cherokee Corn Pones

- serves 8
- 2 cups cornmeal
- ¼ teaspoon baking soda
- 1 teaspoon salt
- ½ cup vegetable shortening
- 3/4 cup buttermilk

- 3/4 cup milk
- butter

Combine cornmeal, baking soda, and salt. Cut in shortening until mixture resembles a coarse meal. Add buttermilk and milk stirring just until dry ingredients are moistened. Form batter into eight 1/2 inch thick cakes. Place on a hot greased griddle (400°F). Cook 15 minutes. Turn and cook an additional 15 minutes. Serve hot with butter.

Indian Fry Bread
Ga-do di-gv-tsa-la-nv-ha a-yv-wi-ya

- 3 cups all purpose flour
- 1 1/2 teaspoons baking powder
- pinch of salt
- 1 1/3 cups warm water
- vegetable oil for frying
- honey

Combine the flour, baking powder, and salt. Add the water and knead the dough until soft. Roll the dough out on a lightly floured board until 1/4" thick. Cut out 4" rounds. Heat 1" to 2" of oil in a saucepan. Fry the bread until puffed. Turn bread when edges are browned on both sides. Serve with honey.

Kanuchi

Kanuchi is a real delicacy to the Cherokee in Oklahoma. A heavy log is hollowed out a few inches in depth. A long heavy stick is used for pounding the nutmeats. The instructions for the making of kanuchi follow:

Hickory nuts, gathered in the fall, are allowed to dry for a few weeks prior to preparation. The hickory nuts are cracked and the largest pieces of the shells are taken out. (Don't worry if small pieces of shell remain in the nuts.) You can pick the larger pieces of shell out by hand or shake the pieces through a loosely woven basket. (You may need to do both.)

Place the nuts into the "bowl" of the log and pound until they reach a consistency that can be formed into balls that will hold their shape. The balls should be about three inches in diameter. Keep the balls in a cool place or freeze them.

When you are ready to prepare the kanuchi for serving, put one of the balls in a sauce pan with a quart or so of water. Bring the water to a boil. (The ball of mashed hickory nuts should dissolve in the water.) Simmer about ten minutes and then strain through a sieve. This separates any of the remaining shell from the nutmeats. The mixture should simmer until it is about as thick as a light cream. Add two cups of hominy to each quart of kanuchi. Most cooks add some sugar or honey. It should be served hot as a soup.

Wild Onions and Eggs

Gathering wild onions in spring is a ritual among the Oklahoma Cherokee. Other tribes who live where these wonderful plants grow harvest them in the spring, also. Wild onions and eggs are often frozen and kept for months so they can be eaten the rest of the year.

Begin with a cup of wild onions that have been cut into small pieces. Two or three tablespoons of bacon drippings are put in a skillet and warmed over medium heat. Simmer and stir the chopped onions in about one fourth cup of water until the onions are tender. If needed, you can add small amounts of water. When the onions are tender and most of the water has cooked away, add six or seven beaten eggs and scramble it all together.

Walnut Mixture

Skin and wash some flour corn in the same way as is done for Bean Bread. Put the corn into a pot and cook until the kernels begin to crack. At this time, you can add raw shelled beans and/or pumpkin. Cook until the beans are soft. While this is cooking, prepare walnut meats by pounding them in the corn beater. Add a little water to the nutmeats. Add the walnut/water mixture to the corn mixture. Cook while stirring constantly for 10 or 15 minutes more. A little meal may be added with the walnut mixture to thicken the dish.

Old Field Apricot Drink

Gather old field apricots. Hull out the seeds and pulp, and put these on to boil after adding a tiny bit of soda to make the seeds separate from the pulp. Strain the juice from the seeds and pulp. Add meal to the juice and cook until the apricots are done.

Leather Breeches

Gather green beans as soon as the beans in the pods mature. Break off the ends and string the pods on a thread or lay them out in a single layer on a sheet. Put the beans in the sun for several days to dry. Bring them into the house at night and during rainy weather. Store for future use by hanging from the rafters or the wall. When ready for use, soak the beans overnight and cook all day the next day. Salt and grease may be added.

Potato soup

Peel white potatoes and cut them into small pieces. Boil in water with one or two onions until the mixture will easily mash. After mashing, add some fresh milk and reheat the mixture. Add salt and pepper if desired.

Squirrel and Hominy

Sa lo li-a le-a ma ge

Clean one squirrel. Roast the cleaned squirrel until done and add to a pot of hominy (white corn). Boil until the meat comes off the bone. Season to taste. Try this recipe the next time you have a Cherokee dinner.

Cornbread

Se-lu ga-du

1/2 cup flour

1/2 cup polenta (coarse ground cornmeal)

1/2 cup regular cornmeal

3 teaspoons baking powder

One heaping tablespoon sugar

Mix dry ingredients, then add:

1-cup milk (Add more milk if needed.)

1 whole egg (slightly beaten)

Mix all together. Preheat oven to 450*F. Slightly cover the bottom of a 9-inch cast-iron skillet or an 8 x 8 inch square pan with oil or margarine. Sprinkle cornmeal in the bottom. Preheat the pan in the oven. Pour in cornbread mix and bake at 450*F until golden brown. This takes about 20 minutes.

Corn Meal Mush

Se-lu i-sa a-ni-s-ta

Corn meal and boiling water

(Use one part corn meal to four parts water.)

Salt the water and bring it to a boil. While beating briskly, slowly add enough cornmeal to make a thick mixture. Cook until the cornmeal is thoroughly done and mushy.

Corn Meal Cookies

Se-lu i-sa u-ga-na-s-da

(This recipe was found in a book dating back to the 1820's.)

Cream together:

    ¾ cup margarine and ¾ cup sugar

Add the following ingredients and stir until smooth:

    1 egg

    1 teaspoon vanilla

Add and mix well:

    1½ cups flour

    ½ cup cornmeal

    1 teaspoon baking powder

    ¼ teaspoon salt

Optional:

    ½ cup raisins

Drop the dough from a tablespoon onto a greased cookie sheet. Bake the cookies at 350°F about 15 minutes. (The cookies should be lightly browned.) This makes about 1½ dozen cookies.

Cherokee Dictionary
Cherokee Syllabary

Da	**R**e	**T**i	**Ꮼ**o	**Ꭳ**u	**i**v
Ꮡga **Ꮉ**ka	**Ꮆ**ge	**Ꭹ**gi	**A**go	**J**gu	**E**gv
Ꮚha	**Ꭾ**he	**Ꭿ**hi	**Ꮀ**ho	**Ꮃ**hu	**Ꮔ**hv
Wla	**Ꮄ**le	**Ꮅ**li	**Ꮆ**lo	**M**lu	**Ꮍ**lv
Ꮵma	**Ꮊ**me	**H**mi	**Ꮈ**mo	**Ꮋ**mu	
Ꮎna **Ꮿ**hna **Ꮐ**nah	**Ʌ**ne	**Ɦ**ni	**Z**no	**Ꮑ**nu	**Ꮕ**nv
Ꮖqua	**Ꮙ**que	**Ꮗ**qui	**Ꮜ**quo	**Ꮜ**quu	**Ꮝ**quv
Ꮒsa **Ꮢ**s	**4**se	**b**si	**Ꮩ**so	**Ꮢ**su	**R**sv
Ꮣda **W**ta	**Ꮥ**de **Ꮦ**te	**Ꮧ**di **Ꮨ**ti	**V**do	**S**du	**Ꮫ**dv
Ꮭdla **Ꮎ**tla	**L**tle	**C**tli	**Ꮬ**tlo	**Ꮯ**tlu	**P**tlv
Ꮳtsa	**Ꮴ**tse	**Ꮵ**tsi	**K**tso	**Ꮷ**tsu	**Ꮸ**tsv
Ꮹwa	**Ꮾ**we	**Ꮻ**wi	**Ꮼ**wo	**Ꮽ**wu	**6**wv
Ꮿya	**β**ye	**Ꭶ**yi	**ꭱ**yo	**Ꮐ**yu	**B**yv

Vowel Sounds

a, as **a** in father, or short as **a** in rival

e, as **a** in hate, or short as **e** in met

i, as **i** in pique, or short as **i** in pit

o, as **o** in note, approaching **aw** as in law

u, as **oo** in fool, or short as **u** in pull

v, as **u** in but, nasalized

Cherokee Syllabary Pronunciation Key

The Cherokee alphabet is written in the syllabary form.

A syllabary is an alphabet in which each letter in a word stands for a whole syllable (such as "ga") instead of a single letter (such as "g"). With the exception of the letter "s," Cherokee is a complete syllabary.

Almost all Cherokee syllables end in a vowel. When using the syllabary, Cherokee words can almost always be spelled as they are pronounced. Spelling sometimes varies when using English letters to interpret the syllables.

The Cherokee language uses the following English consonants:

(d g h k l m n q s t w)

The following English consonants do not exist in the Cherokee language:

(b f p r* t v x z)

The Eastern or lower dialect that is now extinct used a rolling (r) that took the place of the (l) in the other dialects.

A beginning speaker should try keeping the lips still and the mouth slightly opened while pressing the tongue against the lower teeth.

Syllables beginning with (g, except ga) are pronounced almost the same as in English unless used before (k).

Syllables beginning with (d) are pronounced almost the same as in English unless used before (t). (Do, du, and dv) are sounded like (to, tu, and tv) in some words.

Syllables written with (ti), with the exception of (tla), sometimes vary to (di). The syllables (do, du, and dv) are sometimes sounded like (to, tu, tv).

The syllables (qua, que, qui, quo, quu, and quv) are pronounced with a (kw) sound before each vowel.

The syllables (dla, tla, tle, tli, tlo, tlu, and tlv) are pronounced by touching the tongue to the roof of the mouth and then bringing the tongue down as the syllables are spoken. The syllables written with (tl except tla) sometimes are pronounced (dl).

The syllables (tsa, tse, tsi, tso, tsu, and tsv) are pronounced a little differently depending upon the dialect. In Western Cherokee, the syllables are usually pronounced as the (j) in jaw.

Remember to try to keep the tongue at the bottom of the mouth touching the bottom teeth. The (j) sound becomes softer in this way.

At times, Cherokee syllables have unvoiced or silent vowels. At times the silent vowel may be indicated with an apostrophe as in the number seven (ga l' quo gi) or indicated by brackets (ga (li) quo gi). When this happens, the consonant in that syllable is pronounced with the preceding syllable (gal quo gi).

Sequoya
The Inventor of the Tsalagi Syllabary

CHEROKEE DICTIONARY

COLORS & NUMBERS

auburn	da-lo-ni-ge i-yu-s-di
black	gv-nah-ge
black	gv-ne-ga
black	gv-na-ge-i
blue	sa-go-ni-ge
blue	sa-ha-ni
brown	wo-di-ge
color	di-ka-no-di
gray	u-ne-ga e-u-s-ti
gray	u-s-go-lv--sa-go-ni-ge
green	i-tse-hi
green	i-tse-i-yu-s-di
green	i-tse
green	a-tse-hi
ivory	u-ne-gv--go-la
pink	u-s-go-lv gi-ga-ge-I
pumpkin like	i-ya-i-u-sa-ti
purple	gi-ge-s-di
red	gi-ga-ge-i

red	a-gi-ga-ge
red	gi-ga-ge
rose	tsi-s
scarlet	u-s-go-s-da-gi-ga-ge
silver	a-de-lv-u-ne-gv
tan	ga-lv-la-di i-ga-di
white	u-ne-gv
white	u-ne-ga
yellow	da-lo-ni-ge
yellow	da-lo-ne-ga
yellow	da-lo-ni-ge
arithmetic	di-se-s-di
eight	tsa-ne-la
eighteen	ne-la-du
eighth	tsu-ne-li-ne
eighth	tsu-ne-li-ne-i
eighty	ne-la s-go-hi
eleven	so-a-du
fifteen	s-gi-ga-du
fifth	hi-s-gi-ne-i
fifth	hi-s-gi-ne
fifty	hi-s-gi so-go-hi

first	i-gv-yi-i
first	a-gv-yi-yi
five	hi-s-gi
forty	nu-gi so-go-hi-ne
four	nv-gi
fourteen	ni-ga-du
fourth	nv-gi-ne
fourth	nv-gi-ne-i
nine	so-ne
nine	so-ne-la
nineteen	so-ne-la-du
ninth	so-ne-li-ne
ninth	so-ne-li-ne-i
ninety	so-ne-la s-go-hi
number	se-s-di
number	a-se-s-di
numbers	di-se-s-di
one	sa-quu-i
one	sa-wu
one	so-qua
one	sa-quo
one hundred	a-go-hi-tsu-qui

one thousand	sa-quo I-ya-ga-yv-li
one million	i-tsu-qua-di-nv-da
second	ta-li-ne-i
seven	ga-li-quo-gi
seven	ga-li-qwo-go
month	I-ya-nv-da
seventeen	ga-li-qua
seventh	ga-li-quo-gi-ne-i
seventh	ga-li-quo-gi-ne
seventy	ga-li-qua s-go-hi
six	su-da
six	su-da-li
sixteen	da-lu-du
sixth	su-da-li-ne
sixth	su-da-li-ne-i
sixty	su-da-li s-go-hi
ten	s-go-hi
ten	s-go
tenth	s-go-hi-ne
tenth	s-go-hi-ne-i
third	tso-i-ne-i
third	tso-i-ne

thirteen	tso-ga-du
thirty	tso so-go
three	tso-i
three	tso-i
twelve	ta-li-du
twelve	ta-li-du
twenty	ta-li-s-go-hi
twenty-eight	ta-li-s-go tsu-ne-gi
twenty-five	ta-li s-go-hi-s-gi
twenty-four	ta-li s-go-nv-gi
twenty-nine	tali-s go so-ne-gi
twenty-one	ta-li s-go-s-a-qu-u
twenty-seven	ta-li s-go-ga-li-quo-gi
twenty-six	ta-li s-go– su-da-li
twenty-three	ta-li s-go-tso-i
twenty-two	ta-li s-go-ta-li
two	ta-li

DIRECTIONS & MEASUREMENT

above	gah-lay-low (or) ga-lv-la-di-dla
above	ga-lv-la-ti
accrue	u-da-ne-quo-tse-di

acre	su-tli-lo-dv
across	di-ga-na-di-wi-s-sv-i
adjacent	u-da-no-tlv-i
ahead	i-gv-yi-di-tlv
almost	na-v-ni-ge-s-di
aloft	ga-lv-la-di-tlv
among	nu-na-dv-nv
amount	i-ga-i-ge-sv
ample	ye-li-quo i-ga-i
angle	da-s-da-nv-nv--du-lu-tsv
anywhere	yi-ni-ga-li-s-di-ha-quu--i-lv-tlv-i
apart	tsu-ga-le-nv-da
apart	i-yu-da-li
area	e-s-ga-ni (or) i-gv-na-de-na
away	u-tsa-ti-na
back	ga-so-hi
backwards	a-si-ni
behind	o-ni-di-tlv (or) o-ni-di-dla
below	e-la-di (or) e-la-di-tlv
beside	u-li-di-tlv
between	a-ye-li
big	u'-ta-na' (or) e-qua

bigger	u-ta-ni-di
center	a-ye-li
central	i-ga
circle	ga-sa-qua-lv
cold	u (or) u-yv-dla (or) u-yv-tsa
comparison	u-tlo-yi--na-gv-ne-hv
complete	ka-li-wo-hi (or) u-du-lu-la
condition	nu-s-di-da-nv
connection	di-li-go-ta-nv-hi
close	a-s-du-di
cool	u-ne-sv-yv-tli
corner	u-nv-si-yv-i
cross	a-s-ga-si-ti
curve	a-da-yo-hv
deep	a-s-dv-gi (or) ha-wi-ni
degree	i-ga-i--i-ga-ti
direction	ka-lv-gv-I
distance	na-nah-i-yv-i
distant	ge-i
down	e-la-di
down stream	ge-i
east	di-ga-lv-gv-yi (or) nv-da-yi

East	u-la-ga-ha-s-ti
edge	a-s-dv-I (or) si-a-s
end	u-li-s-dv
equal	i-di-ga-di
far	i-nv-hi-yu
fast	ga-tsa-nu-la
fat	u-li-tso-hi-dv
flat	u-wa-na-de-s-gi (or) a-ya-te-ni
foot	su-na-le-i
forward	i-gv-yi-di-tlv
front	i-gv-yi-di-tlv
from	a-ni-gi-s-di---ni-dv-le-nv-da
gallon	so-tlvi-lo-dv
hand width	a-wa-hi-lu
hard	a-s-ti-yi-hu (or) a-s-da-ya
heat	u-ga-na-wu (or) u-di-le-ga
heavy	ga-ge-de-u
here	ha-ya-ni (or) a-ha-ni
high	ga-lv-la-di (or) ga-lv-la-ti
hot	u-di-tle-ga (or) u-de-le-ga
inch	du-no-lv-ta-ni
lean	u-la-tsa-di-u

leaning	ga-lu
left	a-ga-s-ga-ni
level	u-wa-na-de-s-gi
limit	a-se-lv-hi
little	u-s-di (or) u-s-ti
long	ga-nv-hi-da (or) gv-hi-ta
low	ga-lv-a-de-u (or) e-la-di
low	a-la-de-u
measure	a-tli-lo-s-di
middle	a-ye-tli (or) a-ye-li
narrow	a-ya-do-li
near	na-v-i- (or) nu-la-ti
negative	ha-le-nu
none	ka-ni-gi-dv
normal	nu-lo-sv-s-dv-na
North	u
North	tsu-yv-so-li (or) nv-da-de'-wa
off	u-tsa-ti-na
on	na-nah
open	a-s-du-i-dv (or) a-s-du-i-da
opposite	a-hna-di-tlv
out	ga-nv-go-i

outside	do-ya-hi
over	de-li (or) ga-wo-hi-lu-do-di
parallel	du-tso-ta-wa-ti
parched	ga-ha-wi-si-ta
parched	gu-we-su-he
poor	u-le-sa-da-i
quick	u-li-s-da
rate	da-gv-wa-lo-dv
regular	u-tlo-yi-ha
right	du-yu-go-dv
round	ga-sa-qua-lv
short	tsu-s-qua-li
short	u-s-ka-li (or) s-qua-la-i-
side	a-s-qua-ge-ni
size	nu-gv-i
slanting	gu-la-ga-lu
slow	u-s-ga-no-la
slowly	u-s-ga-no (or) lu-s-ga-no-li
slope	a-lu-du-ka-ti
small	u-s-di
soon	na-tla-gu

soon after	a-ni-qua
space	u-dla-nv-dv
South	u-ga-la-ya-i
south	u-ga-no-wv (or) go-ge-yi
square	nv-gi--tsu-nv-si-ya
straight	ga-tsi-ni-s-ta (or) ga-tsi-no-s-du
thick	u-ha-ge-dv
tall	i-nv-i-ga-ti
tall	ga-lv-la-di (or) i-ga-di
test	a-ga-dv-di
top	ga-du-i
turn	a-ga-ta-hv-s-di
under	ha-wi-na-di-tlv (or) ha-wi-ni-tsa
unit	sa-quu-ha
up	ga-lv-la-di
wide	a-ya-te-na
warm	u-ga-na-wa (or) de-la-ka
weight	nu-da-ge-sv
west	wu-de-li-gv-I (or) u-di-li-gv-yi
west	u-sv-hi-yi
West	go-la

after	u-lo-so-nv
after	o-ni
afternoon	sv-hi-ye-yi-di-tlv
afterwards	o-ni u-wa-(ga)-di-di-sv
always	ni-go-hi-lv-i
always	ni-go-hi-lv--i
annual	a-yo-s-do-di
April	ka-wa-ni
April	ga-lo-ni
August	u-la-go-hv-s-di
Autumn	a-ye-li
before	u-da-lu-lv
before	i-gv-yi-di-tlv
begin	a-da-le-ni-ha
day	e-ga
day	v-s-gi-ga
December	v'-s-gi-yi
December	wi-du-yu-go-dv
early	l-lv-yi
early	i-gv-yi-i
early	i-gv-yi

Fall	u-la-go-ho-s-di
Fall	ka-ga-li
February	tsu-nv-gi-lo-s-di
forever	i-go-hi-dv
frequent	i-yu-da-li
Friday	tsu-na-gi-lo-a-ti
Friday	su-tlv-lo-dv
future	u-wa-gu-di-di-sv
Happy New Year	a-li-he-li-s-di i-tse u-de-ti-yv-sa-di-sv-i
hour	e-ya-si-ta-dv-hi
January	de-ha-lu-yi
June	da-tsa-lu-ni
June	gu-ye-quo-:ni
July	a-nv-:yi
late	o-ni-yi-yu
March	a-nu-yi
March	a-(nv)-(i)-s-gv'-ti
May	a-na-s-gv-ti
May	i-ya-ta-wo-s-ta-nv
minute	u-na-do-da-quo-nv-i
Monday	do-da-quo-nv-hi

Monday	u-la-si-de-na
morning	su-na-li
morning	du-ni-nv-:di
night	sv-no-yi
night	i-ga
noon	nv-da-ye-li
noon	u-yv-tlv-i
November	nu-da-de-qua
November	un-a-do-da-qui-de-na
now	no quo
now	na-quu
October	sv-a-yi
Planting Month	a-we-s
Saturday	do-da-qui-de-na
Saturday	ta-li-ni
second	ta-li-ne
second	du-li-:s-di
September	tsu-ga-na-wv
spring	a-ma--ga-nu-go-gv
spring	go
summer	go-gi-a-ye-li
summer	u-na-do-da-qua-s-gv-i

Sunday	do-da-qua-a-gv-I
Sunday	nv-gi-ne-i-ga
Thursday	go-hi-i-ga
time	a-le-ye-su
time	a-li-yi-li-sv
today	su-na-la-yi
tomorrow	su-na-le
tomorrow	ko-hi-u-sv
tonight	go-hi-u-sv-hi
tonight	ta-li-ne-i-ga
Tuesday	ta-la-du i-ya-nv-da
twelve months	tso-li-ne-i-ga
Wednesday	su-na-do-da-qua-s-di
week	wu-de-li-gv
winter	ka-la
winter	su-de-ti-yv-da
year	u-da-ti-ya-hu
year	u-sa-hi
yesterday	u-tlv-hi

MODERN DEVISES

acid	tsu-nu-tso-s-ta
affidavit	a-se-li-ta-nv
airplane	tsi-yu
airplane	tsi-yu ga-no-hi-li-do-hi
almanac	nv-dv-di-se-s-di
alphabet	di-ga-lo-qua-s-do
ambulance	tsu-ni-tlv-go-i-di-ga-lv-do-di
automobile	o-da-mo-qui-li (or) o-da-mo-qui
battery	a-na-ga-li-s-gi
bed	a-tsi-s-ta
bed	ga-ni-tli (or) ga-ni-si
bedstead	ga-ni-tla-di-s-di
bell	a- ha-lu-ni (or) ha-lv-ni (or) u-ha-lv-ni
bench	ga-nv-hi-dv ga-s-gi-lo
binoculars	di-ga-do-di
board	sv-da-lu-ga
boat	tsi-yu
bolt	u-di-qua-lv-de-yi-da
book	go-we-li
book	go

bottle	gu-gu
box	ga-ne-sa-i
box	ka-ne-sa-i
brass	v-tsa-i-yi
brass	tsa-yi
brass	tsu-yi
brick	di-dv-da-nv-hi
bridge	a-sv-tlv-i
bridge	a-sv-tsi
building	a-da-ne-lv
bullet	gu-ni
bullet	ga-ni
bullet	gu-na
camera	di-da-tli-lo-s-do-di
canvas	a-go-li-ye-i-do-s-di
card	a-qua-ni-yo-s-di
carriage	u-s-di--da-qua-le-lu
chain	a-na-da-de-sv-da
chair	ga-s-gi-na
chair	ga-s-gi-lo
chimney	a-hu-tsa-wa-la-gv-i
clock	wa-tsi

compass	a-la-ni a-ga-da-di
computer	e-li-s
curtain	a-ya-do-la-dv-di
cushion	a-s-gi-lu-di
desk	di-go-we-lo-di
dictionary	di-de-tlo-qua-s-do-di
dime	s-go I-ya-da-nv-te-di
drawer	a-sa-hi-s-di
drill	de-ta-le-s-ti
electric	a-na-ga-li-s-gi
e-mail	i-me-lv
engine	a-tsi-lv--a-ni-gi-s-gi
flats	di-ya-te-ni
frame	ga-lv-do-di
glass	a-do-ge-di
glass	u-ne-s-da-la
glue	di-ka-nv-wo-di
gun	ga-lo
gun	ga-lo-que
gun	u-nu-da-na
gun sheath	a-yv-du-la-di
hammer	ga-nv-qua-lo-s-di

hammer	ga-ne
hammer	gv-ni-li-da-s-da
handsaw	u-s-di- ga-na-do-gi
hay rake	ka-na-s-ga a-gi-s-do-di-gv-gi
hymn book	di-ka-no-gi-s-di go-we-li
ink	ga-ne-hi-di--go-we-lo-di
instrument	go-hu-s-di--gv-ta-ni-da-s-di
insurance	gu-da-lv-do
Internet	ka-na-ne-s
key	s-di-i-s-di
lamp	a-tsv-s-di-go-i-
letter	gi-lo-ni-da-yu-nv-nv--go-wi-li
lock	da-ga-si
match	a-tsu-s-di
mattress	a-tse-s-do
metal	ta-lu-gi-s-gi
money	a-de-la
nail	yv-gi
needle	ga-ye-wi-s-do-di- yv-gi
newspaper	di-ga-le-yv-ta-nv-hi go-we-li
nickel (coin)	hi-s-gi i-ya-da-nv-te-di
oil	go-i

paper	go-we-li
parcel	ga-que-nv-hi
paste	ga-ya-lv-di
pencil	li-go-we-lo-di
pillow	a-gu-s-do
plow	ga-da-lu-go-di
pump	ga-sa-do-ya-s-gi
receipt	ka-no-hv-s-gi--a-gi-sv
record	go-we-lv
sheet	u-ta-no-hi
steel	a-tsi-lu-ta-lu-gi-s-gi
stove	a-da-s-da-di ga-ka-hv-i-
table	ga-s-gi-lo
table	a-li-s-da-yv-di
telephone	di-li-no-he-di
telescope	a-ka-ta-ti
ticket	a-yv-s-do-di
train	di-ga-tsa-nu-la
truck	ga-na-sa-ne-s-do-di
web site	ka-na-ne-s-ga u-si-li-de-wi-sv nu-s-da
wire	u-ya-nv-hi

TOOLS & SUPPLY

adz	de-ga-nu-da-s-ti
ammunition	di-s-da-yo-s-do-di
anvil	go-tlv-(nv)-di-a-tlo-di
anvil	a-so-di ta-lu-gi-s-gi u-li-gi
arrow	di-ga-da-tlv-da (or) da-ka-le-da-ti
arrow	gu-ni (or) ga-tli-da
arrow shaft	ga-nu-s-ta da-ka-le-da-ti
arrowheads	di-a-ga-da-tlv-da tsu-s-go
ashes	ga-s-du (or) go-s-du
awl	de-ta-la-s-ti
ax	u-dv-na ga-lu-ya-s-ti
ax	ga-lu-ya-s-ti a-gi-ya
ax	ga-lu-ya-s-ti u-s-di (or) ga-lu-ya-s-ti
badge	a-ka-ne-s-di
bag	de-ga-lo-di (or) ga-nv-dv-I
bait	ga-?di
ball	a-la-s-ga-lo-di (or) gu-na
ball	a-ne-tsa (or) a-ne-tsa u-na-s
ball	a-ne-tsa ta-ga-lo-de
barrel	sv-do-ni
base	a-le-nv-di-s-gv

blowgun darts	gi-tsi
bow	ga-tso-di
bow	ga-li-tsa-di
bow	ga-lo-tsa-di
bow and arrows	ga-tso-di a-le go-ni
bow and arrows	ga-tso-di a-le gu-ni
bow string	ga-tso-di da-di
broad ax	u-dv-na ga-lu-ya-s-di
broom	gv-no-sa-s-di
brush	ga-nu-go-nv-do-di
bucket	ta-lu-gi-s-gi go-yi-nu-s-di a-ma
bucket	a-ma--gu-gi-s-do-di
candle	u-ka-na-wi a-tsv-s-do-di
canoe	tsi-yu
catgut	di-s-ta-i'-yi
charcoal	gi-na-s-gi
container	a-tli-s-do-di
cord	u-ni-qua-te-na--a-s-di
dipper	di-ta-ti
doll	a-ne-lo-di
doll	a-na-lo-di
dolls	da-ne-lo-ha-s

door	a-s-du-di
door	ga-lo-hi-s-di
drum	a-hu-li
fireplace	ga-do-di-yi
fireplace	a-tsi-la-yi
fireplace	go-dv-di a-hu-tsa-wo-la-dv-i
fish net	de-sa-di
fish trap	u-ga-yv
flag	ga-da-ti
flax	a-ta-le-ta
flint	da-wi-s-ga-la
flint	ta-wi-s-ka lv-ti
floor	a-ya-te-no-hi
floor	a-ya-di-tla-hu
foot log	a-sv-tli
foot log	a-sv-tlv-yi
hatchet	ga-lu-ya-s-ti
hatchet	da-na-wa ga-lu-ya-s-ti
hoe	ga-la-ga-di
hook	su-di
horn	tsu-lu-nu-hi
horn	u-yo-na

Indian ball sticks	a-ni-ya-wi-ya-I di-la-s-ga-li-di
knife	ha-ya-la-s-ti
knife	gv-hi-ya-la-s-ti
knife	ha-ye-la-s-di
knot	da-ka-ne-hv
litter	a-ni da
medicine	nv-wo-ti
medicine	nv-wa-ti
medicine	nv-wa-ti
net	ga-ya-lu-di
net	da-su-du-di
oar	ga-ga-wa-s-ti
paint	a-si-wi-s-ti
pouch	da-ga-tli
punk	ta-wa-li
quilt	ye-ga-li
rattle	ga-na-tse-di
rattle	ga-na-se-ti
rod	ga-nv-hi-d--ta-lu-gi-s-gi
spear	da-da-s-do-di
stick	ga-na-s-da
stool	a-li-s-dv-tsu-di ga-s-gi-lo

storehouse	a-da-na-nu-hi
tassel	u-tsi-tsa-lu
teepee	a-ni-gv-wi-ya--u-ni-la-tso-dv
teepee (cloth)	a-na-wo a-da-ne-lv
teepee (skin)	ga-ne-ga a-da-ne-lv
tent	ga-li-tso-da-di
thong	ga-no-tsi
tin	s-gu-o
tomahawk	ga-lu-ya-s-di
tray	a-tla-nv-da-di
wagon	da-qua-le-lu
war club	a-ta-si
war paint	wo-di
war pole	a-ta-de-da-wa-s-do-di
war stick	a-da-s
wax	a-dla
wheel	ga-qlua-do-di
whip	ga-wa-s-dv-ni-s-di
window	tso-la-nv
window	tso-la-ni

PLACE & LOCATION NAMES

abode	ga-ne-lv
America	a-me-li-ga
anywhere	ni-gv-quo
apartment	de-ka-nv-su-lv
Arkansas	yo-wa-ne-gv
avenue	ga-la-nv-dv
avenues	de-ga-la-nv-dv
barber shop	di-da-s-do-di-yi
ballground	a-ne-tsa ga-da
bank	a-de-lv--di-di
Big Cove	go-la-nv-yi
Birdtown	tsi-s-quo-hi
Bloody Ground	go-na-da gi-ga-ha-i
Brier Place	ka-nu-gu-la-yi
building	a-ne-s-ge-ha
Bullhead	u-s
camp	su-s-ti-yi
cave	u-s-ta-ga-la-yi
ceremonial mound	i-tsa-ti
Cherokee	tsa-la-gi-yi
Chota	tsv-ge-yi

Chunky yard	**da-ni-la-wi-ga**
church	**di-ga-la-wi-i-s-di**
church	**tsu-ni-la-wi-s-di**
church	**si-ti**
Council House	**a-ni-tsa-la-gi-ga-do-hi**
country	**do-yi-di-tlv-ga-du-hv**
country	**u-ge-da-li-yv-i**
cove	**a-sa**
crossing place	**de-tsa-nv-li**
Darkening Land	**a-wi'-s'**
Deerhead Cove	**tsu-s-gi-na'-i**
enemy country	**u-ga-do-hi**
farm	**ga-lo-ge-sv**
ford	**a-sa-tsv-yi**
fort	**a-ni-ya-s-ka nv-a-yu-da**
garden	**a-wi-sv-sv**
garden	**a-wi-sv-di-yi**
Ghost Land	**go-na-da gi-ga-ha-i**
heaven	**ga-lv'-la-ti**
highway	**e-qua-nv-no-hi**
hollow	**u-sv-do-ni**
home	**di-tse-nv-sv**

home	tsu-ne-nv-sv-i
home	di-que-nv-sv
home	di-que-nv-sv-i
home	tsu-ne-nv-sv
home	di-tse-nv-sv-i
home	tsu-we-nv-sv
home	e-hu
home	ga-la-tsa-di
hospital	tsu-ni-tlv-gi--u-na-ni-tlv-di
hot house	a-si
house	ge-tsa-di
house	ga-la-ta-sa-di
house	ga-li-tso-de
house	a-da-ne-lv
hunting grounds	ka-na-ti-yi
Kentucky	go-wi-li--de-ga-nv-di-go-li-ye-di
library	a-ma ye-li-gv-hi-ta
log cabin	tsu-lv-da-ge-wi a-ne-s-gv-di
Long Island	ta-li-de-na-da-ga-nu
Lookout Mountain	gu-wa-hi
market	u-ni-na-di-nv-di
Mulberry Place	da-gu-na-yi

Mussel Shoals	da-gu-na-we-la-hi
Nashville, Tennessee	na-tsi-yi
Natchey Town	nv-ya-gi
New York	o-ga-la-ho-mi
office	di-ga-lv-wi-s-da-ne-di
Oklahoma	tsi-ya-hi
Paint-town	a-mo-ga-da u-tsa-na-ti
Paint-town	ni-wo-di-hi
passageway	ga-ne-nu-tlv-i-
path	nv-ne-hi
pigeon place	wa-yi
Pine Log	na-sv-tli
Pine Log	na-tsi-a-sv-tlv-yi
Qualla	qua-lv-yi
race course	v-ta
Rattlesnake Springs	ga-ni-da-wa-s-gi
Rattlesnake's Master	e-la-wa-di-yi
Red Clay	a-ma-ga-yv-hi
road	nv-no-hi
Running Water	o-da-lv-?i no-ya
Saluda	se-lu-di-yi
Sand Mountain	tsa

school	di-de-lo-qua-s-di
Sitico	u-tsu-ti-qua-yi
Smoky Mountains	gu-li-se-tsi-yi
Snowbird	gu-li-se-tsi-yi
Snowbird	du-di
Soco	sa-quo
station	u-le-we-s-di
store	a-da-na-nv
storehouse	a-da-na-nu-hi
street	ga-la-nv-dv
Sugar Town	wa-ta-u-ga
sweatlodge	a'-si
Sycamore Shoals	te-na-si
Tennessee	e-qua-ni-ma-ya
Tennessee	ta-ni-si
Tennessee River	nv-da-gi
Texas	ta
Toccoa	da-tsu-na-la-s-yv-yi
town	ga-du-hv
trail	nu-nah-i
trail	u-s-di nv-no-hi
Trail of Tears	u-lv-yi

Trail of Tears	nv-na-da-u-la-tsv-yi
Trail of Tears	ge-tsi-ka-hv-da a-ne-gv-I
Tuckaseegee	a-mo
Tuckaseegee	da-ga-si-yi
Tugaloo	gv-na-ga
Tuscola	ta-s-go-la
United States	a-ma ye-li
Wolf-town	wa-yo-hi
Yellow Hill	e-la-wo-hi

Cherokee Stories

In the beginning...

When all was water, the animals lived above in Galunlati, but it was very crowded. They wanted more room. Dayunisi, the water beetle, offered to go see what was below the water. The water beetle repeatedly dived to the bottom and came up with soil eventually forming the island we call Earth. Cords at each of the cardinal points of the sky vault that is solid rock suspended the island.

Birds were sent down to find a dry place to live, but none could be found. The great buzzard, the father of all buzzards we see now, flew down close to Earth while it was still soft. He became tired. His wings began to strike the ground. Where they struck the Earth, a valley was formed. Where they rose up again, the Earth became a mountain. Thus, the Cherokee country was created.

The animals came down after the Earth dried, but all was dark. So, they set the sun and attached it to go every day across the island from east to west. At first, the sun was too close to the island, and the island was too hot. They raised the sun again and again for seven times until it was the right height. The highest place, Gulkwagine Digalunlatiyun, is "the seventh height."

The animals and plants were told to keep watch for seven nights, but as the days passed, many began to fall asleep until the seventh night only the owl, panther, and a couple of others were still awake. These were given the power to see in the dark and prey on the birds and animals that sleep at night. Of the plants, only the cedar, the pine, the spruce, the holly, and the laurel were awake on the seventh night. Therefore, they were given the power to be always green and to be greater medicine than the others. It was said to the other plants, "Because you did not endure to the end, you shall lose your hair every winter."

Man came after the animals and plants. At first, there were only a brother and a sister. The brother struck his sister with a fish and told her to multiply. So it was. In seven days a child was born to her, and thereafter, every seven days another child was born until there was danger that the world could not keep up. It was made that a woman should have only one child in a year. And, it has been so ever since.

The Origin of Strawberries

When the first man was created and a mate was given to him, they lived together very happily for a time. Then, they began to quarrel. At last, the woman left her husband and started off toward "Nundagunyi," the Sun Land in the East. The man followed alone and grieving, but the woman kept on steadily ahead and never looked behind. "Unelanunhi," the great Apportioner (the sun), took pity on him and asked him if he was still angry with his wife. He said that he was not, and "Unelanunhi" asked him if he would like to have her back again. He eagerly answered, " Yes."

So, "Unelanunhi" caused a patch of the finest ripe huckleberries to spring up along the path in front of the woman, but she passed by without paying any attention to them. Farther on, he put a clump of blackberries, but these also she refused to notice. Other fruits and some trees covered with beautiful red berries were placed beside the path to tempt her, but she still went on until suddenly she saw in front of her a patch of large ripe strawberries, the first ever known. She stooped to gather a few to eat. As she picked them, she chanced to turn her face to the west and all at once the memory of her husband came back to her, and she found herself unable to go on. She sat down, but the longer she waited the stronger her desire for her husband became. At last, she gathered a bunch of the finest berries and started back along the path to give them to him. He met her kindly, and they went home together. [viii]

Why Rabbit Has a Short Tail

(As retold by Barbara Shining Woman Warren)

A very long time ago in the young days of the world, Rabbit had a very long bushy tail. The truth is that his tail was longer and bushier than Fox's tail. Rabbit was so very proud of his tail that he was constantly telling all the other animals about how wonderfully beautiful his tail was. But, the day came when Fox became weary of hearing Rabbit brag about his beautiful tail. So, he decided to put an end to Rabbit's boasting once and for all.

The weather was getting colder and colder. One day, it finally became so very cold that the waters of the lake and the streams froze. A few days later, Fox went down to the lake carrying four fish. When he got to the lake, he cut a hole in the ice. He tied those four fish to his tail, and then he sat down and waited for Rabbit to come.

Soon, Rabbit came hopping over the top of the ridge. When Fox saw Rabbit, he quickly dropped his tail into the cold water. Rabbit hopped right up to Fox and said, "What are you doing?"

"I'm fishing, Rabbit," Fox replied.

Rabbit said, "How long have you been fishing?"

Fox lied and said, "Oh, only about 15 minutes."

"Have you caught a fish yet?" asked Rabbit. Then, Fox pulled up his tail, and there were those four fish hanging on to it.

Rabbit said, "Fox, what do you plan to do with the fish you catch?".

Fox said, "Well, I figure I'll fish for about a week. Then, I am going to take all those fish down to the Cherokee village and trade them for a pair of beautiful tail combs. There is only one set of tail combs left, and I really want them." Fox could see that Rabbit was thinking.

Rabbit thought to himself, "If I fished all night long, I bet I would have enough fish by morning to trade at the

Cherokee village. Then, I could get those tail combs for myself."

Fox said, "It's getting late, and I'm cold. I think I'll come back and fish some more in the morning. I'll see you later rabbit." Then, Fox loped off over the top of the ridge. As soon as Fox was out of sight, Rabbit dropped his tail down into the icy water of the lake. Brrrr, it was cold!

But, rabbit thought, "Oh, no. I want those tail combs more than anything." So, he sat down on the hole in the ice and fished all night long.

Soon after the sun came up, Fox loped over the top of the ridge. He ran right at Rabbit. He said, "What you doing there, Rabbit?"

Rabbit's teeth began the chatter. "I'm ffffissssshing, Ffffox."

"Have you caught a fish?" Fox inquired.

Rabbit started to get up, but he found he couldn't budge. He said, "Fffox! You've ggot to helppp me. I'mmm sssttttuck."

So Fox, with a big smile on his face, walked behind Rabbit. He gave Rabbit one mighty big shove. Rabbit popped out of that hole and landed clear across the other side of the lake, but his tail was still stuck in the frozen water. And, that's why from that day to this day; Rabbit has such a very short, short tail.

How the Milky Way Came to Be

(As retold by Barbara Shining Woman Warren)

Long ago when the world was young, there were not many stars in the sky. In those days, the people depended on corn for their food. Dried corn would be made into cornmeal by placing it inside a large hollow stump and pounding it with a large wooden pestle. The cornmeal was stored in large baskets. During the winter, the ground meal could be made into bread and mush.

One morning an old man and his wife went to their storage basket for some cornmeal. They discovered that someone, or something, had gotten into the cornmeal during the night. This upset them very much for no one in a Cherokee village stole from someone else.

Then, they noticed that the cornmeal was scattered over the ground. Giant dog prints were in the middle of the spilled meal. These dog prints were so large that the elderly couple knew this was no ordinary dog.

They immediately alerted the people of the village. It was decided that this must be a spirit dog from another world. People did not want the spirit dog coming into their village. They decided to get rid of the dog by frightening it so bad it would never return. They gathered their drums and turtle shell rattlers, and later that night, they hid around the area where the cornmeal was kept.

Late into the night, they heard whirring sounds like many birds' wings. They looked up to see the form of a giant dog swooping down from the sky. It landed near the basket and began to eat great mouthfuls of cornmeal.

Suddenly, the people jumped up beating their drums and shaking their noisemakers. The noise was so loud; it sounded like thunder. The giant dog turned and began to run down the path. The people chased after him making the loudest noises they could. The giant dog ran to the top of the hill and leaped into the sky, the cornmeal spilling out the sides of its mouth. The giant dog ran across the black night sky until it disappeared from sight, but the cornmeal that had spilled from his mouth made a pathway across the sky. Each grain of cornmeal became a star.

The Cherokees call that pattern of stars, "gi li ut sun stan un yi" (gil-Lee-oot-soon stan-Unh-yee), "the place where the doll ran."

And, that is how the Milky Way came to be.

The Legend of the Cedar Tree

(As told by Jim Fox)

A long time ago when the Cherokee people were new upon the earth, they thought that life would be much better if there was never any night. They beseeched the Creator that it might be day all the time and there would be no darkness.

The Creator heard their voices and made a ninth season. It was daylight all the time, and the forest became thick with growth. It became difficult to walk in the forest and find the path. The people toiled in the gardens many long hours trying to keep the weeds pulled from among the corn and other food plants. The Earth got hot, very hot, and continued that way, day after long day. The people began to find it difficult to sleep and became short tempered and argued among themselves.

Not many days had passed before the people realized that they had made a mistake. And, once again, they beseeched the Creator. "Please," they said, "we have made a mistake in asking that it be day all the time. Now, we think it should be night all the time." The Creator considered this new request and thought that perhaps the people might be right even though all things were created in twos representing day and night, life-and-death, good and evil, and times of plenty and times of famine. The Creator loved the people and decided to make it night all the time as they had requested.

The day ceased and the night fell. Soon, the crops stopped growing. It became very cold. The people spent much of their time gathering wood for their fires. They could not see to hunt meat and with no crops growing, it was not long before the people were cold, weak, and very hungry. Many of the people died. Those that remained alive gathered once again to beseech the Creator. They cried to the Creator, "We have made a terrible mistake! You had made a day and a night perfect and as it should be from the beginning. We ask that you forgive us and make the day and night as it was before."

Once again, the Creator listened to the request of the people. The day and night became as the people had asked, just as it was in the beginning. Each day was divided between light and darkness. The weather became more pleasant, and the crops began to grow again. Game was plentiful. The hunting was good. The people had plenty, and there was not much sickness. The people treated each other with compassion and respect. It was good to be alive. The people thanked the Creator for their lives and for the food they had to eat.

The Creator accepted the gratitude of the people and was glad to see them smiling again. However, during the time of the long days of night, many of the people had died, and the Creator was sorry that they had perished because of the night. The Creator placed their spirits in a newly created tree. This tree was named "a-tsi-na tlu-gv" (ah-see-na loo-gah), the cedar tree.

When you smell the aroma of the cedar tree, gaze upon it standing in the forest and remember that if you are Cherokee, you are looking upon your ancestor.

Tradition holds that the wood of the cedar tree holds powerful protective spirits for the Cherokee. Many carry a small piece of cedar wood in a medicine bag worn around the neck. It is also placed above the entrances of homes to protect against the entry of evil spirits. Traditional drums are made from cedar wood.

Do today's Cherokee believe in this legend? Well, let's just say that there is a piece of cedar in my medicine pouch, and I wear it always. The Creator did not make the people because of loneliness. He made them in order to show generosity and love to the people. Accept the blessings in the gifts given, and always give thanks for them.

(Jim lives in Alabama. Visit his website at:

www.Angelfire.com/AL2/gaasaguali/index.html)

Two Wolves

One evening, an old Cherokee told his grandson about a battle that goes on inside all people. He said, "My son, the battle is between two 'wolves' inside us all."

"One is Evil. It is anger, envy, jealousy, sorrow, regret, greed, arrogance, self-pity, guilt, resentment, inferiority, lies, false pride, superiority, and ego."

"The other is Good. It is joy, peace, love, hope, serenity, humility, kindness, benevolence, empathy, generosity, truth, compassion, and faith."

The grandson thought about it for a minute and then asked his grandfather, "Which wolf wins?"

The old Cherokee simply replied, "The one you feed."

Genealogy Research and the Amazing Journey

(By Elder Cindy Jarrell "Cherokee Rose")

In researching your ancestral history, always begin with the present and work your way back to the beginning of your time. You do not research from the past to the present; you research from the present to the past. So, in order to find your ancestors, you will need to begin with yourself. Record your birth information and your parent's names including your mother's maiden name, places and dates of birth, and places and dates of marriage. Then, proceed back in time entering the same information regarding your grandparents and on back. You can search on the Internet through free search sites such as:

www.rootsweb.com

www.familysearch.org

www.cyndislist.com

www.heritagequest.com

www.usgenweb.org

Other websites charge a fee for research. Some of these sites are listed below:

www.ancestry.com

www.footnote.com

Sometimes, I simply type key words for the information I am seeking into www.google.com. Many times the resulting information is informative, but sometimes it is not. Free pages for recording the information you gather may be obtained at www.rootsweb.com. At the top of the search bar under a heading for *Other Tools and Resources*, you will find blank forms. You can find family group sheets and pedigree sheets. These free forms can be printed. Also, you can go to your local genealogy center and request forms for recording ancestral information.

The best way to start gathering information is with records of births and deaths. Before 1940, in some of the smaller towns, births were not always recorded. In many states, death records were not recorded prior to 1914. Many smaller, rural communities did not register death records until after the 1930's. Marriage records were recorded in the white man world in very early times, but the Native American people had their own methods of recording documents. This method did not include the courthouse or public documentation.

Family Bibles can be an excellent source of information, but not all families owned a Bible. If the families did own a Bible, it may not have survived to make it to your hands. Unfortunately, many Native Americans were not acquainted with the Bible.

Other information can be obtained from Indian Rolls, census records, wills, probate records, land records, immigration records, military and pension records, school records, and church records. Still, you may not find anything pertaining to your ancestors. Many schools were started for the Native Americans, and they were forced to attend those schools. There may be some school records; but once again, the way the white man recorded and the way the Indians recorded history were different. Your ancestors may have used their Indian names. Unless you know the Indian language, you may never know who they were.

By pinpointing the location in which your last known relatives were living, if it was before the 1900's, you can obtain information by studying the migration pattern. Most Native Americans followed a pattern of migration that followed a major source of water. The waterways played a major roll in the Native American's existence.   Use your computer, library, or genealogy center to locate waterways and the names of Indian tribes that utilized those areas. This will aid you in determining from which tribe your family originated. Also, determine when the white man entered the area you are searching. For example, in the state of Tennessee, the first white child was born around 1757. So, if your ancestors were in that area prior to that date, they must be of Indian ancestry. Missouri did not allow Indians to live in the state after approximately 1837. (However, some of my ancestors did live in the area and were known as white or "Black Dutch.")

I am constantly searching for answers to the basic questions of who, where, when, and why. Who was the person I am researching? Where did they live? When did they live there? Why do you think they have Native American blood?

Then, of course, comes one of the most difficult parts of research, which is sorting out the family stories and tales. Just because his family and neighbors called a person "chief," doesn't necessarily mean he was an actual chief. Nor, does the fact that a many times removed grandmother wore her hair in braids mean she was Native American. Just because you were told that one of your grandmothers was an Indian princess doesn't mean that she was Native American, either. Many family tales are just simply family tales. Likewise, simply being dark-skinned, dark-eyed, or black-haired doesn't mean you are a Native American, either. You may just be a dark-skinned, black-haired descendant of European ancestors. Any of the above information could be a clue; or, it could indicate that you just simply must look for more facts. Not everyone is descended from notable chiefs, maidens, or even a president. The family tales have nothing to do with the fact that you could, or could not, be a Native American. You might be Native American; but maybe, just not from the royal line. Still, your ancestry is just as important as any family's ancestry that indicates they descended from a royal line. You can still proudly claim your heritage whatever the case.

Check all the Indian rolls. If you do not find your ancestors named on them, you might still be Indian. They may not have walked the Trail of Tears. Your ancestors may have already been where they intended to be without any government help. Or, they could have simply fled in fear of their family's safety and to avoid being told what to do by the white man.

Many Indian girls married white men so they would have a "so called" better life, or so the tribe would have a white person to help them in their every day living. Times were very difficult, and many Native Americans made sacrifices to protect their loved ones and help them have a safer and better life. Marriage among the Native Americans and whites were common and resulted in the cultures of both races being intertwined. Hundreds of marriages occurred in some families, which of course, distresses some of our modern folks to no end. Just think about all of those cousins marrying one another. I have come to feel that there are likely several factors involved in this situation. If you hear or find the term in-bred, don't get hysterical. We don't want to think that it would have occurred in our family. However, it is very possible that it happened among most of our families at some point in time.

Intermarriages were much more common among the Europeans than Native Americans. However, intermarriages have been going on since the beginning of time; just read your Bible. It may have begun as an attempt to keep "the blood" within the family, but it may have also involved the family's societal position. Those families with similar socioeconomic circumstances married among themselves. It is also likely that it may have involved their membership in certain church denominations. They may have been encouraged to marry within a certain circle. More than likely, all of these and some other factors are involved. Another repeated occurrence worth mentioning is that whites that had been adopted by the Indians tended to marry one another after returning to their original families.

Most of us have heard the terms Black Dutch, Black German, and even Black Irish. These were terms used by the Native Americans to hide their Indian ancestry. This was done, not because they were ashamed of who they were, but it was done in fear for the safety of their families. Most Native Americans were honorable and very proud people. If someone claimed to be Native American, they were not allowed to buy, sell, trade, or own property for many years. Many feared the white man and did not want harm to come to their families.

I believe it is vital for those of us who are of Native American descent to know who we were, who we became, and the ways we have survived. With many Native Americans forced to live on reservations and others being adopted into other tribes, we, as a people, have been forced to adapt. Some Native Americans disappeared only to reappear as mountaineers, hillbillies, or as members of isolated or nearly isolated groups near the bottom of the socioeconomic ladder. Many Native Americans have risen to great heights among the whites. Some have astounded the world with their success.

My opinions may differ from others. However, my curiosity has led me in a journey back through time and allowed me to locate many forefathers of my own and others. I hope this information will help you discover your past as well as your future. Researching genealogy is "time travel" with endless, fascinating destinations. Hopefully, you will enjoy finding your ancestors, learning the area in which they lived, and their methods of survival. Appreciate where you truly came from. Best of luck in all your ventures!

Genealogical Research

(By Tom "Red Feather" Ward)

Genealogy is not difficult to do, but it will take time, patience, and finances to be able to accomplish your goal of finding your roots. Genealogy will take you places that you have never been, and many times, you will find information that you would rather not have known.

In genealogical research, you start with yourself and work backwards. You must document anything and everything that you can about your family. Keep copies of everything. From personal experience, I have discovered that it is wise to place your important documents on a compact disc of some type. Original records can be lost or destroyed. Once you lose a record or document, it may be difficult to recover that particular record again unless you have a copy elsewhere. There are genealogy programs available in various stores and on websites that will also help you to organize and store your information.

When searching for records, it is always prudent to use at least two different sources to back up your research. For instance, a census record, a land transaction, a will, probate records, etc., can all be valuable assets to you. Free genealogy forms are available by using a simple search engine. I might point out that sometimes only one record may exist, such as a family Bible or journal. These are considered to be the most accurate information and are considered to be "authoritative" as a family member who would have had knowledge of the information wrote them.

In genealogy, you start with what you know and work backwards. Start with your birth certificate. This will show your parent's names and many times it will show their places of birth. If your parents are living, obtain copies of their birth certificates. Their birth certificates will show their parents and possibly where their parents were born. If your parents married under the legal age, look for a copy of their marriage license, as most marriage licenses will be recorded in the county where the marriage took place. If your parents or grandparents are deceased, then obtain a death certificate and obituary. These items will give you a lot of information.

Trying to actually document your "Indian" heritage may, or may not, be possible. The reason for this is because many places, such as the state of Missouri, outlawed Indians from living in the state. They were not allowed to own property and didn't even have voting rights. To be an "Indian" was considered to be lower than dirt. Many of our ancestors had to deny their heritage just to stay alive and keep their families alive.

Be persistent. You will not find everything you are looking for in one day. There are genealogy websites, such as Rootsweb.com, where you can find information on your family. Contact genealogical societies or search library records in the area where your ancestors lived. You will find people who are willing to help you research. You may have to pay a few dollars for copying and mailing items to you, but you will find that the cost is well worth the expense.

I might also point out that when finding information on the Internet, try to contact the person who posted the information. Ask for their source. Search the sources they list and verify their information, unless of course, you know the person and trust their research.

Good luck in your search. May the Great Spirit guide you into all truth.

The Seven Cherokee Clans

Elder Ben "Little Eagle" Stephens's grandmother passed this information down to him. A list of clan member's names is included. This information is very valuable for searching out your ancestry. It can be used as a tool in determining your clan.

Cherokee society is a matrilineal society. This means clanship is attained through the mother. Prior to Oklahoma becoming a State, women were considered the heads of the households with the children belonging to them in a situation where the husband and wife separated. The knowledge of a person's clan is important for many reasons. Historically, and still today among Cherokee traditionalists, it is forbidden to marry within your clan. Clan members are considered brothers and sisters. In addition, when seeking spiritual guidance and Indian doctoring, it is necessary to name your clan. Seating at ceremonial dances is by clan, as well.

Among the Cherokee there exist seven clans or families. These clans are:

AniSahoni (Blue Clan) - Those belonging to this clan are keepers of all children's medicines and caretakers of medicinal herb gardens. Historically, this clan included many people who were able to prepare special medicines for the children. They became well known for a medicine produced from a bluish colored plant called a "blue holly" and were so named after this plant. This clan has also been known as the Panther or Wildcat Clan in some regions. They are known as a White (Peace) Clan. Their color is blue, and there wood is ash. The totems of the Blue Clan are turquoise, blue jay, black willow, blue clay, sourwood, otter, and holly.

Some family names once associated with the Blue Clan are:

Choltoskie, Yansa Gatoga, Roap, Fawling, Tlunduski Gureega, Wadichacha, Burns, Raven, Lame Arm, Shallelock, Oolutsa, Skellelock, Kena Teta, Big Fellow, Bent Leg, Bear Tracker, Cowin, Quatisis, Roy, Mankiller of Settico, Tacite, Ooloostah, Gilideehee, Pohatan Oolashela, Drowning Bear, Canaughkutt, Brown, Lowery, Silver Walker, Dardrene, Talontaskee, Burns, Walker, Bannon, Dull Knife, Dare, Deehee, Duck, Bradberry, Ray, Sagoni, Geegah Nundah, Marlin, McKinnley, Niven, Mackintyre, Rose, Griss, Lewis, Heard, Hair, McCoy, McKenney, Gray Horse, Inlow, Koffr, Goforth, Red Hand, Bearfield, Buzzark, Crouch, Gains, Gates, Grundy, Kinder, Blood, Chambers, Miller, Ross, Hobbs, Bushy, Green, Ballew, Boling, Ableman, Rogers, Blue, Silver Bear, Revels, Casteel, Danials, Starr, Baker, Long, Turner, Rains, Blue Horse, Dog, Proper, Zion, Lock, Young, Bear Striker, Good Pasture, Foreman, Zilliox, Yates, Yager, Peters, Kickupp, Cornseen, White Beaver, Ballard, Alberty, Poor, Highfield, Kitchen, Loudermilk, Hamby, Hare and Wilson.

AniGilohi (Twister Clan) – The Twister Clan has also been known as the "Long Hair" Clan. (*Note*: AniGilohi – Gilohi is short for the ancient word Gitlvgvnahita, the warrior women's Society, meaning "something that grows from the back of the neck."). Angilohi was a very peaceful clan. Our chiefs usually came from this clan at one time in our history. The clan color for AniGilohi is yellow, and their wood is beech. The totems for the Twister Clan are snowy egret, red cedar, cutworm, rattlesnake, coyote, and river cane.

Some family names once associated with the Twister Clan include:

Due, Rogers, Judd, Coody, Martin, Grant, Bushy Head, Price, Two Speaker, Awneeyuhlah, Jumper, Cornsilk, Larch, Walking Stick, Corntassel, Fields, Grout, Emory, Buffington, Emory, Dardeen, Coffy, Fairweather, Buzzard, Blevins, Hare, Hardmush, Bearfield, Cash, Heard, Duck, Goodpaster, Coin, Casada, Burk, Ballew, Bentleg, Breedlove,

Stockton, Gibson, Berry, Burr, Kagama, Martin, Alderman, Turpine, Fallin, Bryant (*My Family*), Lane, McMinn, Ball, Dean, Palmer, Storm, Reeves, Owens, Turnback, Strikes, Mann, Williams, Welch, Twister, White Hair, Donolee, Izzard, Griffin, Casteel, Neal, Rogers, Harris, Light, Johnson, Webber, Siegart, Beaver, Burkhart, Augus, Silk, White Hair, Eads, Highcloud, Casada, Lane, Turner, Northrup, Red Bone, Arnold, Strayhorn, Red Snake, Red Crow, Raincrow, Coal, Little, Old Fellow, Moss, Richie, Puckett, Quayugi, Glass, Gillbin, Gillmore, Black, Bear Paw, Blaze, Christe, Talquetta, Stump, Courtney, Hare, Turnbo, Coffey

AniTsiskwa (Bird Clan) – Those belonging to this clan are the keepers of the birds and sacred feathers used in bird medicines. The belief that birds were messengers between the people and Creator gave the members of this clan the responsibility of caring for the birds. They were messengers and were very skilled in using blow guns and snares for bird hunting. The members of this clan originally presented eagle feathers, as they were the only ones allowed collecting them. Their color is purple, and there wood is maple. The totems of the Bird Clan are the bat, carp, yellowhammer flicker, flying squirrel, green fly, and dogwood.

Some family names once associated with the Bird Clan are:

Ghigooie, Shorey, McDonald, Brashears, Old Tassel, Sinnawah, Eades, Jarrett, Thomas, Jimmesen, Eagle, Brown, Oowodagee, Gossey, Starr, Bolin, Pigion, Bell, Barr, Red Eagle, Young Bird, Toy, Turky, Stalking Turkey, Frost, Gibson, Quail, West, Love, McDaniel, Reid, McCraken, McCrigger, Perry, Lipe, Light, Boss, Cutting, Alred, Webb, Brownwater, Waters, Owl, Rainwater, Otter Lifter, Moss, Bird, Baker, Cody, Cunningham, Justice, Fields, Field, Burning Twing, Choate, Reynolds, Ray, Davis, Rogers, Angus, Bean, Arkensas, Alexander, Adair, Daloneegah, Kee, Ewers, Finley, Pool, Fair Hair, Rains, Miller, Moore, Hill, Sanders, Terripin, Cooper, Byles, Grant, Scott, Daughtrey, Bunch, Red Crow, Negro, Mayes, Little, Scofield, Hull,

Cuthand, Feather, Leukins, Ketcher, Jordan, Burk, Raincrow, Barr, Crouch, Leflor, Kingsnake, Cousart, Goingbird, Donedeesdee.

AniWodi (Paint Clan) – Members belonging to this clan made red paint. Members of the Paint Clan were historically known as prominent medicine people. Medicine is often "painted" on a patient after harvesting, mixing, and performing other aspects of a ceremony. They were the smallest and most secretive clan. When the Cherokee would wage war, the priests would bring along several sacred objects, medicinal herbs, and a coal from the sacred fire. They were the only ones that were allowed to make a special red paint and dye that were used for ceremonial purposes and warfare. Because of this, they were considered a Red (War) Clan. The clan color for the AniWodi is white, and their wood is locust. The Paint Clan's totems are sassafras, paint stone, snapping turtle, redbird, staghorn beetle, bloodroot, and red clay.

Some family names once associated with the Paint Clan are:

Candie, Craft, Easten, Ebanoy, Lee, Ohmaohla, Sassafracs, Tohquah, Jolly, Telontaskee, Mankiller, Woods, Berry, Watts, Caulunnah, Tassel, Pumpkin Boy, Nettle Carrier, Colbert, Shaman, Tuskiehoo Toh, Colbert, Double Head, Taliwuasku, Gist, Churchfield, Byrd, Hard gritts, McCoy, Adair, Cummins, Artt, Berryhill, Bunch, Face Painter, Morrison, Richardson, Rickhart, Teal Duck, Breamer, Sasadeehee, Redd, Poolay, Hartley, Quintin, Simons, Quinley, McDougal, Gillam, Keeper, Keep, Towle, Goforth, Chandis, Gillam, Foose, Kingsman, Snapping Turtle, Linder, Hollow Horn, Jump, Proctor, Knight, McKissic, Yellowhammer, Stephens, Taylor, Kettle, Cash, Turnkey, Yahne, Samuals, Riddle, Roundtree, Macky, Williams, Stone, Sparks, Redman, Porkeater, Hudson, Parrot, Polson, Manystriker, Reily, Ligon, Sharp, Ulam, Underhill, Gann.

AniKawi (Deer Clan) – Those belonging to this clan were the keepers of the deer, deer hunters, trackers, tanners, and seamers, as well as keepers of the deer medicines. Members of the Deer Clan were historically known as fast runners, foot messengers, and hunters. Even though they hunted game for subsistence, they respected and cared for the animals while they were living among them. They were known as messengers on an earthly level. They delivered messages from village to village and person-to-person. They were considered a White (Peace) Clan. The clan color for the AniKawi is brown, and their wood is oak. The totems of the Deer Clan are squirrel, red ant, redheaded woodpecker, mudstone, white deer, and oak.

Some family names once associated with the Deer Clan are:

Kingfisher, Spain, Matt, Madstone, Squrril, Blackburn, Cook, Cline, Short, Burnthand, Jones, Wilhort, Workman, Mann, McMorea, McCubbin, Mayfield, Vance, Spicer, Stacie, Page, Puffett, Reddstone, Scruggs, Told, Wing, Whiteside, Weston, Stray Horn, Troutman, Tin Cupp, Stalecup, Tucker, Thimble, Ketcher, Arkensaw, Custalow, Longstrider, Teacup, Lipe, Owens, Jackson, Spain, Nigro, Pigion, Pardue, Nephi, Silver, Salesman, Jolly, Horn, Jumper, Crow, Cole, Quealy, Sample, Sharp, Tacket, Wail, West, Adams, Corwin, Cowin, Inlow, Lynch, Martin, Bryant, Kickupp, White Doe, White Deer, Price, Gist, Lowry, Starr, Kingfisher, Ward, Blevin, King, Blaze, Doty, Pucket, Langly, McKenney, Grundy, Bearscamp, Coalman, Wiggans, Swiftbird, Polsome, Short, and Stephens.

AniGatogewi (Wild Potato Clan) – Historically, members of this clan were known to be keepers of the land, farmers, and gatherers. They were named after the wild potato plants they gathered in the swamps (hence the name "gatogewi" -- Swamp) and along streams to make flour or bread for food. The Wild Potato Clan has also been known as the Bear Clan, Raccoon Clan, and even Blind Savannah in different regions. They were a White (Peace) Clan. The clan color for the AniGatogewi is green, and there wood is birch. The totems of the wild potato clan are slippery elm, black cougar, rabbit, mole, raven, obsidian, corn, and brown bear.

AniWahya (Wolf Clan) – The Wolf Clan is the largest clan today and the most prominent. This clan provides most of the war chiefs and warriors. Wolves are known as protectors, and the Wolf Clan are protectors of the people. The Wolf Clan members are keepers and trackers of the wolf and the only clan who could kill a wolf through special ceremonies and wolf medicines. They are known as a Red (War) Clan. The clan color of the AniWahya is red, and their wood is hickory. The totems of the Wolf Clan are terrapin turtle, white pine tree, coneflower, mica, wild Turkey, and hornet.

Some family names once associated with the Wolf Clan are:

Hicks, Canoe, Broom, Little Owl, Long Limper, Inlow, Highstriker, Forbush, Coseen, Fire Carrier, Custalow, Badger, Turkey At Home, White Mankiller, Ooneeghdeehee, Little Fellow, Tsiyugigaghy, Tame Doe, Nionee, Linsey, Foose, Coughmann, Sheepkiller, Dragging Canoe, Ward, Longfellow, Nancy Ward, Tranquatti, White Dog, Dull Knife, Grundy, Highpine, Chandler, Doekiller, Bradberry, Black Fox, Bugg, Sain, Walkes, Rider, White, Starr, Caudle, Hill, Towie, Boxturtle, Straw, Littlefield, Coin, Turtle, Bowl, Keener, Beaver, Atkins, Bell, Raiper, Cupp, Lowery, Allen, Tucker, Blades, Adams, Atkins, Oldham, Easton, Mackey, James, Sam, Stephens, Todd, Wolfe, Huganen, Nution, Bloom, Gann, Neil, Neal, Watie, Boodinaugh, Ridge, Whitehorn, Brown, Tucker, Fale, Hand, Coxs, Coateney, Hilderbrand, Wood(s), Long, Grite, Thimble, Wade, Wise, Riddle, Sharp, Uhlery, Kirtch, Kickupp, English, Action, Abercrombie, Bledsol, Parks, Mills, Holt, Taylors, Hale.

The Lord's Prayer

o-gi-do-da ga-lv-la-di-he-hi

Our father, heaven dweller,

Ga-lv-quo-di-yu ge-se-s-di de-tsa-do-v-i

My loving will be (to) Thy name.

Tsa-gv-wi-yu-hi ge-sv wi-ga-na-nu-go-i

Your Lordship let it make its appearance.

a-ni-e-lo-hi wi-tsi-ga-li-s-da ha-da-nv-te-s-gv-i

Here upon earth let happen, what you think,

Na-s-gi-ya ga-lv-la-di tsi-ni-ga-li-s-di-ha

The same as in heaven is done.

Ni-da-do-da-qui-sv o-ga-li-s-da-yv-di s-gi-v-si-go-hi-i-ga

Daily our food give to us this day.

di-ge-s-gi-v-si-quo-no de-s-gi-du-gv-i

Forgive us our debts,

Na-s-gi-ya tsi-di-ga-yo-tsi-na-ho tso-tsi-du-gi

The same as we forgive our debtors,

a-le tla-s-di u-da-go-le-ye-di-yi ge-sv wi-di-s-gi-ya-ti-nv-s-ta-nv-gi

And do not temptation being lead us into,

s-gi-yu-da-le-s-ge-s-di-quo-s-gi-ni u-yo ge-sv-i

Deliver us from evil existing.

Tsa-tse-li-ga-ye-no tsa-gv-wi-yu-gi ge-sv-i

For Thine your Lordship is,

Tsa-tse-li-ga-ye-no tsa-gv-wi-yu-gi ge-sv-i

And the power is,

a-le e-tsa-li-gi-di-yi ge-sv-i

And the glory is forever.

e men

Amen

End Notes

[i] Roy S. Dickens "The Origins and Development of Cherokee Culture." In *The Cherokee Nation*, edited by Duane H. King. Knoxville: University of Tennessee press, 1979.

[ii] John Ehle - *Trail of Tears, the Rise and Fall of the Cherokee Nation* – Anchor Press, 1988

Elmo Ingenthron - 1970 the Western Cherokees. In *Indians of the Ozarks Plateau*, chapter 7. The school of the Ozarks rests, point Lookout, Missouri.

Cephas Washburn, 1869 reminiscence of the Indian's. Reprinted by Kew Park 1955 - the Press Argus, Van Buren, Arkansas.

Hester A. Davis – "The Cherokee in Arkansas: an invisible archaeological resource." In *visions and revisions: at no distorted perspectives on Southern cultures*, edited by George Sabo III and William Schneider. Southern Anthropological Society Proceedings 20. Athens: University of Georgia press, 1987

[iii] http://www.tolatsga.org/Cherokee2.html

[iv] *United States v. Old Settlers*, 148 U.S. 427, 13 S.Ct. 650, 37 L.Ed. 509 (1893)

[v] http://www.tolatsga.org/Cherokee2.html

[vi] http://www.prophecykeepers.com/chickamaugacherokee/westerncherokee.html

[vii] http://www.cherokeebyblood.com/recipes.htm#A

Brown, John P. Old Frontiers. (Kingsport: Southern Publishers, 1938).
Conley, Robert J. The Cherokee Nation: A History. (Albuquerque: University of New Mexico Press, 2008).
Hoig, Stanley. The Cherokees and Their Chiefs: In the Wake of Empire. (Fayetteville: University of Arkansas Press, 1998)
McLoughlin, William G. Cherokee Renascence in the New Republic. (Princeton: Princeton University Press, 1992).
Mooney, James. Myths of the Cherokee and Sacred Formulas of the Cherokee. (Nashville: Charles and Randy Elder-Booksellers, 1982).
Moore, John Trotwood and Austin P. Foster. Tennessee, The Volunteer State, 1769-1923, Vol. 1. (Chicago: S. J. Clarke Publishing Co., 1923).
Wilkins, Thurman. Cherokee Tragedy: The Ridge Family and the Decimation of a People. (New York: Macmillan Company, 1970).

[viii] History, myths and sacred formulas of the Cherokee by James Mooney